WHAT EVERY RUSSIAN KNOWS
(AND YOU DON'T)

WHAT EVERY RUSSIAN KNOWS
(AND YOU DON'T)

OLGA FEDINA

Anaconda Editions

Published by Anaconda Editions, 2013

Copyright © Olga Fedina

British Library Cataloguing-in-Publication Data
A catalogue record for this book is available from the British Library

ISBN 978 1 901990 12 6

www.whateveryrussianknows.com

Anaconda Editions
27 Sage Way
London WC1X 0PQ

email: editions@anacondaeditions.com

Cover design and photo: Al Lapkovsky at Begemotfoto
www.begemotfoto.com

CONTENTS

Acknowledgements

This book was conceived from initially half-formed ideas, occasional bouts of nostalgia and a desire to explore aspects of Russia which friends and students had found intriguing or perplexing. Above all, it grew from the generous help of many people.

From chats with Marina Cosmetatos and Svenja Erich, reminiscing about those crazy times in 1990s Moscow.

From lessons with my Russian language students, and particularly Michael Gore and Simon Calvert, whose enthusiasm for Soviet and Russian popular culture gave me the idea to write this book.

From Raj Yagnik's generous help, patiently reading and ruthlessly commenting on the first drafts.

From email correspondence with Bill Foreman on Mikhail Bulgakov.

From John Maher's overall involvement in the book, especially his help with all those pesky definite and indefinite articles in the English language, and his support and forbearance as my husband.

I am very grateful to two outstanding writers and experts on Russia and the Russians, Vanora Bennett and Michele A. Berdy, for their help in shaping this book, and for their generous comments and encouragement.

Thanks are also due to Camelia Ovezea for her enthusiastic support and for creating the website (www.whateveryrussianknows.com) for the book, to Pierpaolo Palazzo for the author photograph and to Al Lapkovsky from Begemotfoto for the cover illustration and design.

And most of all to Robert Thicknesse, the editor of this book, who has been overwhelmingly generous with his time and Russian expertise, guiding me through the writing process and constantly challenging me (with a sometimes heady cocktail of severity and support).

To all the people I have not mentioned in person (from friends and relatives to journalists and bloggers I've never met) who gave me ideas and inspiration – thank you.

Foreword

I first turned up in Soviet Russia at the impressionable age of 18, not long after the invasion of Afghanistan and a month after the controversial Moscow Olympics. To describe what followed as a culture shock would be an understatement. My hotel, on the very edge of Moscow, had just been built for sports fans, and you reached it by walking over a building site full of still unused giant pipes, though already, in the manner of somewhere on the Costa del Sol, the doorknobs and taps in the rooms were falling off. It was a blisteringly hot summer, with mosquitoes. The food was always cold, the waiters grumpy, the barmen at the hotel disco overinterested in my actions in what often seemed the wrong way, and "real" people in the outside world of Moscow strangely cagey about hanging out with foreigners. Yet, however alarmed my family and friends felt about my trip into this Evil-Empire enemy territory, I was gloriously confident that Moscow could hold no terrors for me. Chekhovian characters would be bound to pop out from under the pipes, I reasoned; there would be wistful dialogues in *dachas*, over tea, with wolves howling somewhere far off in the forests; and I would understand everything. Didn't I have four years of studying behind me, after all, and an A-level that proved I was conversant with the poetry of Pushkin and the more arcane uses of the Russian gerundive?

Like many other foreigners, I was then (briefly) charmed to discover that all Moscow taxi drivers, benefiting from the rigorous Soviet education we'd heard so much about in the West, could also recite the love lyrics of Pushkin, and often did. "I loved you once," we would chant happily at each other, as they accelerated down enormous streets empty of everything but a distant trolleybus, "it may well be/That love has not died yet…"

Other friends and other entertainments gradually followed. And yet, on that trip and many, many subsequent visits to Russia over the years – culminating in my working in Moscow for seven years in the very capitalist 1990s – my imperfect knowledge of pre-Soviet Russia, while always very politely applauded, turned out not, after all, to be quite the Open-Sesame into modern life that I'd hoped for.

Like many foreigners in Russia at that time, I subscribed to the patronizing belief that Russians, brought up without the capitalist advertising that had given my generation of English speakers a whole informal vocabulary of jingle-speak, must have missed out on, and been impoverished by the lack of, a popular culture. Yet I couldn't help but notice that there was another cultural world everyone I met in Russia always seemed to be referring to – one that, even with the university degree in Russian I'd got by now, remained deeply obscure to me for many years more. What's more – and this really seemed a mystery wrapped in a riddle inside an enigma – when the history of Soviet Russia seemed to have been so laden with tragedy for so long, what was it that people here were always laughing about?

I just didn't get why people kept snuffling with glee when they'd answer what I'd thought was a straightforward question with something surreal like, "oh, there was shooting…" or grinning like lunatics when I asked why a Central Asian-themed restaurant serving raisin rice and kebab in a muddy Moscow street went by the unlikely name "White Sun of the Desert."

If only I'd had Olga Fedina's brilliant book in my hand back then, how much easier solving the riddle of Russia would have been. For Fedina has done all foreign Russia-lovers an extraordinary service by, at last, letting us in on that long-running private joke. Written with a delightful blend of wit, affection, mockery and restraint, her book is a reminder of how much more there was to those 70 Soviet years than just hard times, teeny-weeny unspendable banknotes and rubbish cars. *What Every Russian Knows (And You Don't)* is a guide to Soviet-era films, music, people, books – not to mention the subversive jokes, subtexts, dodges, inventiveness and sheer human bloody-mindedness – which, right through a century in which it might have been easier to give up and cry, kept people in the Russian-speaking world smiling. You'll probably never understand today's Russia without this guide to the pleasures of a part of the past that we in the West have mostly ignored. Luckily, you no longer need to.

Vanora Bennett, *author and journalist*

PREFACE

When I was working as a Russian teacher I taught students of all levels. Some of them spoke very good Russian, having done a Russian degree. They knew a lot about Russian classical literature and could recite Alexander Pushkin's poem "The Bronze Horseman" by heart in Russian

> *Na beregu pustynnykh voln*
> *stoyal on, dum velikikh poln...*

But despite this feat of memory, like students of foreign languages in general, they were at sea with references from popular culture, films, songs, novels and animated cartoons. These are the source of innumerable quotations used by Russians every day; Russians recognize them immediately and know where they came from.

It's one thing to learn a language, another to acquire the frame of reference that underpins the language. Of course, this is a vast and constantly-changing thing, and one can never hope to encompass it all, but I hope that for students of Russian and anyone interested in Russia it will be instructive and useful to read about the classics of popular culture that have lodged themselves in the national psyche and the language.

This book aims to outline the cultural hinterland of people like me who grew up in late Soviet times, focusing on things that are still watched, read and listened to. It cannot aim to be comprehensive, and my compatriots may argue about the choice of subjects. The subjects I have chosen are not necessarily the best things that were ever produced in the USSR, but they have proved to be the most durable.

***

What is the secret of their success, why do they continue to permeate the day-to-day life of the Russians? I think this is because these films, books, animated cartoons and personalities have proved the ones that most effectively helped people to cope with the world around them, both in Soviet times and afterwards.

Living in an experimental state with its own peculiar system, fenced off from the outside world, somewhat lost in time, in an oppressively controlled society, gave rise to unusual ways of dealing with reality.

You could try to beat the system, like Ostap Bender. You could hope for a sparkle of New Year magic to break through the drabness of the everyday, as in the film *The Irony of Fate (or, Enjoy Your Bath!)*.

You could end up believing only in yourself and nothing else, weary of the demands of heroism and the inscrutable world, like Sukhov and Vereshchagin in the film *White Sun of the Desert*.

You could opt for non-resistance, going with the natural flow of things, discovering the magic behind the natural world, like Yemelya the Simpleton in the fairy tale.

You could take on reality, paying a high price in the process, as happened to the singer-songwriter Vladimir Vysotsky. Or you could dismiss anything that did not concern everyday problems, like the characters in the film *Moscow Does Not Believe in Tears*.

You could withdraw into the melancholy world of the imagination, watching the twilight by a samovar and counting stars, like Hedgehog and Bear Cub in the animated cartoon *Hedgehog in the Mist*. Or you could escape into a jolly world of friends, animals and fresh country air, as in another animated cartoon, *The Prostokvashino Three*.

You could even create your own "abroad", finding comfort in the familiarity of a reinvented Victorian England, as in the TV series *Sherlock Holmes and Dr Watson*.

You could ask questions: do things have to be the way they are? – as the comedian Mikhail Zhvanetsky does. Or you could reject and mock the way things are, like another comedian, Mikhail Zadornov.

Or the world around you could suddenly be transformed, giving you a mystical insight that made you feel "invisible and free", such as many felt when reading *The Master and Margarita* by Mikhail Bulgakov.

The Soviet Union has gone, but the reality of post-Soviet capitalism requires of Russians that they rely on their long-established coping skills. Post-Soviet popular culture has not produced its uniform and uniting frame of cultural references. So, the old movies, books and personalities endure and still help us to deal with the world around us.

✯✯✯

This book aims to give you a fuller understanding of Russian and the Russians – and you will be able to say, like Ostap Bender, the indomitably opportunistic hero of the satirical Russian classic *The Twelve Chairs*, when a new idea hits him: "The ice has cracked, gentlemen of the jury! The ice has cracked!" – "Лёд тронулся, господа присяжные заседатели! Лёд тронулся!" (translations from the Russian throughout the book are by the author)

THE IRONY OF FATE (OR, ENJOY YOU BATH!)

ИРОНИЯ СУДЬБЫ, ИЛИ С ЛЁГКИМ ПАРОМ!

New Year's Eve in Russia can be a stressful day. Cooks are hoping not to be hit by a power cut just as they put the pies in the oven as the electricity grid is overwhelmed with demand. Young people are wondering how to manage both to please their families and get to central Moscow in time for the street parties. Businessmen are feverishly trying to remember whether they have confused their presents for their long-suffering wives with those for their 18-year-old girlfriends. The president is getting ready to persuade the people in his New Year's speech that the dawning year will be at least a little bit better than the one that is finishing.

Every new year is unpredictable. This is doubly true in Russia, where – as comedian Mikhail Zadornov said in the 1990s, when the KGB's archives were being opened and previously unknown facts exposed – not just the future but the past, too, is unpredictable. But one thing is certain: every year on 31 December on Russian TV at least one channel will show the three-hour long 1975 film *The Irony of Fate, (or Enjoy Your Bath!) (Ирония судьбы, или С лёгким паром!).*

The film's plot is this: it is New Year's Eve in 1970s Moscow. The protagonist, Zhenya Lukashin, a 30-something doctor who lives with and obeys his mother (a completely normal situation in Russia) is for the first time preparing to celebrate the New Year with his fiancée, a bossy and possessive young woman. The doctor is shy and scared of commitment, but it seems that now he is finally about to tie the knot.

However, he has other obligations, too. Every year his friends and he go to the *banya* (steam-bath) together. This is a tradition he cannot break, not even for his fiancée.

"To Zhenya's wedding!", "To Zhenya's fiancée!", "To friendship!", "To the bachelor life!" – in the *banya* one toast follows another until the men get completely plastered. The two who have managed to stay conscious remember that one of the lads was supposed to be flying to Leningrad. But which one? They decide it must have been Zhenya, and get him on a plane.

On the plane he spends his time sleeping on the shoulder of an irritated passenger and poking his face with a bundle of birch twigs (which *banya*-goers use to lash one another with to get the muck out of the pores). This irritated passenger (played by the film director Eldar Ryazanov) grumpily helps our hero off the plane in Leningrad. Still half-asleep, Zhenya gets in a taxi and gives the driver the address: 3rd Builders' Street, block 25, flat 12. "Четвёртый этаж" – "Fourth floor", he adds as he is falling asleep again. "Хоть пятый" – "Fifth, if you want," replies the taxi driver, with the deadpan irony of taxi drivers everywhere.

Zhenya arrives at his destination; the streets are lined with typical, endless, identical Soviet tower blocks. He could be in any Soviet city. He enters the building, the key fits in the lock, the Polish furniture in the flat is much the same as his. It seems only that someone has moved it around, but our hero is still too drunk to pay much attention. He gets into bed and falls asleep... only to be found and woken up by the beautiful Nadya, a schoolteacher preparing to celebrate New Year's Eve with her serious, well-to-do and extremely jealous boyfriend, who, in her heart of hearts, she does not love, but... she is 34 and the years are flying by. And Ippolit – the boyfriend (the actor Alexander Yakovlev, who I insist looks just like John Cleese, though readers may disagree) – is so dependable, and gives her presents of "real French perfume".

This is how the story unfolds... And I will not say any more, because you must see this film, and I do not want to spoil it for you.

The opening credits immediately reveal how packed it is with star names.

The director, Eldar Ryazanov, is one of Russia's most popular filmmakers. His first film, in 1956, was *Night of the Carnival (Карнавальная ночь)*, which immediately made him famous. He subsequently made a couple of dozen brilliant films, including *Beware of the Car (Берегись автомобиля)* and *Office Romance (Служебный роман)*, mostly comedies (although always with a serious, or even tragic, streak). A man of charisma and bubbling energy, in the 1980s and 1990s his immediately recognizable stout figure was ubiquitous on television, whether as presenter, interviewer or interviewee. Ryazanov is now in his 80s, living in Moscow and still making films, even though he always swears to God he will retire after the next movie.

The protagonist, Zhenya, is played by Andrei Myagkov, one of Ryazanov's favourite actors, no doubt for his brilliant interpretation of an ordinary, shy, "insignificant" person, the Soviet "little man", who, when faced with extraordinary circumstances, has to show his extraordinary qualities. Eldar Ryazanov said about Myagkov: "To play a person drunk to unconsciousness and still remain natural, likable, and funny is an incredibly hard task. Myagkov does it easily and with flair. To undress, get into somebody else's bed and be rude is not very difficult. But to stay charming and amusing while doing that, and to evoke the love of the public – this is something not everyone can achieve."

Because of his everyman looks, the actor says he can still pass unnoticed on Moscow's public transport, despite appearing in many very well-known and much-loved movies. Every Russian knows Myagkov as the drunken doctor from *The Irony of Fate* (the actor says he was so fed up with being associated with this particular role, he even came to dislike the *banya*). But people also remember him as Tolya Novoseltsev, a quiet single father statistician from Ryazanov's *Office Romance*, who rises up to fight for his love and the dignity of his friend. Or as the elder Turbin brother in *The Days of the Turbins* – *Дни Турбиных*, Vladimir Basov's film based on Bulgakov's novel *The White Guard*. Not everyone remembers that one of Myagkov's first roles was Alyosha in the 1969 version of *The Brothers Karamazov*, which was nominated for an Oscar for best foreign-language film that year.

Barbra Brylska, who played the beautiful occupier of the Leningrad flat, has become a household name in Russia thanks to this one film. However, it seems that this role has hindered rather than boosted her career as an actress in her native Poland. Some say this was because of the anger of the Polish public and cinema community at her receiving an award from the Soviet government for *The Irony of Fate*. She says the reason was envy at her success. In the film she was dubbed by a Russian actress, as her Polish accent would have been noticeable.

When she is singing the voice actually belongs to Alla Pugachova, then a thin, shy and not-so-well known singer. Having made it big soon after the film came out, Pugachova has been a megastar for the last 25 years, not just for her singing but, especially in later years, also for her appearances in celebrity gossip TV shows.

Mikael Tariverdiev, who wrote the music for the film, is a serious classical composer (and a student of Khachaturian) who subsequently became better known for writing music for numerous films, many of them very famous. The film is full of ballad-style songs to lyrics by Yevgeny Yevtushenko, Bella Akhmadulina, Marina Tsvetayeva – all wonderful and well-known poets.

The film was a huge success with the public immediately on being shown in 1975, and year after year, as families prepare to celebrate New Year, they watch this film. Russians who live abroad are very likely to have it on DVD.

When I lived in Moscow, I watched *The Irony of Fate* as everyone would – between chopping the boiled carrots, potatoes, chicken, gherkins and eggs for the *olivier* salad, an indispensable dish on the New Year table. Knowing the plot by heart, you could start watching it at any point, get distracted, then come back again.

This film is a perfect Soviet Christmas fairy tale. In the atheist Soviet Union New Year's Eve replaced Christmas as a family holiday with the decorated tree and children getting their presents. After the collapse of the Soviet Union, and with the rediscovery of Christmas, New Year's Eve still occupies a much more important place in the life of the Russians. It probably has something to do with the fact that Russian Orthodox Christmas falls on 7 January, so it is celebrated after New Year and not before. That, and the lack of a Christmas tradition, have led to 7 January being treated mainly as a day of rest from the excesses of the New Year period.

As for 25 December, nothing happens in Russia on that day at all. A Spanish friend of mine found himself alone in Moscow one ("Western") Christmas day. He surrounded himself with bottles of *champanskoe* and sat down, confident that his friends, knowing his girlfriend was away and he was on his own, would call and invite him to celebrate Christmas with them. Time passed and nobody called. Finally, he started phoning people, only to hear bemused questions about why 25 December was so special, and why he expected festivities. Of course, this wouldn't have happened in Moscow on New Year's Eve.

But, getting back to our film – what is it that has made it such a beloved Christmas fairy tale for more than a generation of Russians?

The director takes quite a conventional plot, a comedy of errors. In a typical romantic comedy narrative device, two lonely people are brought together in unusual circumstances, and end up spending New Year's night together.

This story is set against the background of 1970s Moscow; the mid-70s, since labelled the "Era of Stagnation". This was the hangover after the excitement of the 1960s: the Khrushchev "thaw", a time of creativity, poetry and hope, when after Stalin's death it seemed as though the Soviet Union could come to terms with and repent its awful past, and become a different and renewed state. In the 1970s the country sank quickly into a grey decade of bureaucratic state rule and the triumph of mediocrity.

But, even under those circumstances, human feelings survive, and people are still able to believe in magic, that everything can be new and different, and that a twist of fate on New Year's Eve can connect people who have been unconsciously yearning for each other. The mixture of the real and unreal, the magic of Russian winter with its snow, fur hats and the smell of Christmas trees, the poetry and the prose of day-to-day life...

Taking the film from comedy into drama and back into comedy, the director and his crew created a perfect fairy tale through that mysterious film-making alchemy that is so hard to achieve, or to replicate on purpose.

The protagonists of this film are not the usual Soviet "heroes": they are not tractor drivers going off to plough virgin lands to give the country more grain; not Arctic explorers withstanding hellish conditions to advance Soviet science; nor farmers who harvest 3,000 tons of wheat instead of the 1,000 tons they are required to gather according to the Five-Year Plan. The protagonists are slightly chaotic, weak-willed city dwellers, both living with their mothers, both lost in the world and not very happy. Moreover, Zhenya has a terror of commitment and Nadya is a dreadful cook.

Some Westerners, when they first see this film, are surprised that something so subversive was not only allowed to appear under the Soviet regime, but was shown on TV every year. The film starts with an animated cartoon showing an architect looking contentedly at his project for a new apartment block. In the process of going from one bureaucrat's door to another, the draft loses all its original features one by one, until by the time it is approved all that is left is a typical Soviet rectangular apartment block. The film is not only making fun of the uniformity of Soviet aesthetics ("In the old days, finding himself in a strange town, a person would feel lonely and lost. Everything around was strange: different houses, different streets, different life. And now it is a different matter! You go to any town for the first time and you feel at home!"). It also points out the uniformity of thinking, the greyness of day-to-day life where a miracle can happen only on New Year's Eve.

Oddly, none of this ever gave the film censorship problems in the USSR. Ryazanov did have trouble getting government sponsorship (the only sponsorship available in the Soviet Union) because the storyline of this film was seen as being apolitical, and the story of a drunken doctor finding love when landing in the wrong city was regarded as lacking a moral lesson.

It is ironic that this film was indeed banned for a couple of years, but this occurred during *perestroika* or, to be more precise, Gorbachev's anti-alcoholism campaign of 1985–87, when it was deemed to be promoting drunkenness.

This campaign is not very well-known in the West. But in Russia Gorbachev is very much remembered for his (needless to say, unsuccessful) attempts to reduce alcohol consumption by diktat, and one of his nicknames in Russia is "Lemonade Joe" after the protagonist of a comic Czech Western, a cowboy who drinks nothing but lemonade. As tends to happen in Russia (and many other places, too, as far as I can see), what sounded like a good idea quickly fell victim to the law of unintended consequences. The lack of available vodka led to the widespread production of *samogon*, homemade hooch of varying quality (some not properly distilled and literally deadly) and the complete disappearance from food shops of the sugar which was needed for this purpose. Many vineyards in the south of Russia, Ukraine and Georgia were destroyed, some containing unique varieties of grapes. A leading expert on wine and grapes, Pavel Golodriga, seeing the fruit of his life's work ploughed under, committed suicide.

Scenes where characters were drinking alcohol were cut from movies during the campaign. With *The Irony of Fate* this would have been difficult, given that without the drunkenness scene it would be hard to justify the protagonist's sudden relocation to Leningrad. So the film was simply not shown for a couple of years.

Apart from this prohibition-related problem, one thing that surprises you watching Ryazanov's films, and thinking about the times when he made them – from the late 1950s onwards – is that his work wasn't more assiduously censored. The impression one gets is that under the Soviet regime he was somehow able to do exactly what he wanted. Many of his films seem so critical of Soviet reality that you wonder how they were ever allowed to be shown. But this effortlessness is superficial. Ryazanov later on admitted in an interview that every time he made a film he had to "squeeze a slave out of myself and overcome my fear of the Soviet authorities". Westerners, when getting acquainted with Soviet-era culture, are sometimes surprised to find that many satirical works of art wriggled through the censorship. The idea that the West has of the Soviet Union as a totalitarian state does not make much distinction between the Stalin era and the – not exactly liberal, but certainly less harsh – times that followed. Moreover, the satirical exposure of the "shortcomings" and "diseases" of society (such as alcoholism, bribery, bureaucracy) was officially encouraged as it was seen as a way of getting rid of these "shortcomings".

One of Ryazanov's most satirical works is *The Garage (Гараж)*. For those who want to get an idea of what life was like in the USSR, in terms of stereotypical characters and relationships between people, there is no better guide than this movie.

At what appears to be a routine meeting of a cooperative-built parking complex it is suddenly announced that the city authorities are about to build a road right by the prospective garage. That means four parking spaces will have to go, and after months of waiting, helping at the building site and forking out "unexpected expenses", four members will have to go back to the end of the queue.

So who will the four be? The governing board of the cooperative has already decided. They will be the four most inoffensive, quiet, "little" people who can easily be got rid of. Everyone but the four gives out a sigh of relief, and is ready to vote in favour and go home.

But one of the four rises up against this injustice, a "little man" with a scarf round his neck (played by – you guessed it – Andrei Myagkov). Because of a bad cold, he has lost his voice, but this does not prevent him from standing up to the majority.

Many archetypes of Soviet life are there. A hard, severely-dressed female communist party official. A glamorously high-heeled meat market director. The despairing wife of a "loser", someone who is always the first to be overlooked. An eminent professor whom life has taught to be careful with the authorities. The son of a big *nomenklatura* official, languid and decadent. A Second World War veteran, who suddenly and painfully realizes that, while he had thought nothing of fightning behind German military lines, he is now afraid to say a word against the bigwigs of the garage cooperative. A single mother, tiny, slight and fragile who dares to raise her voice for justice. And a voiceless (here literally, because of his cold, as well as, of course, metaphorically), unremarkable little man, who suddenly finds himself incapable of tolerating the unfairness and rises up against it.

I could not resist the temptation to digress and tell you more about *The Garage*, a less well-known film by Ryazanov. But let us get back to *The Irony of Fate*. Apart from being satirical and funny, this film has sad overtones, mostly in the songs. All the songs in this movie are sad, and they are all about loss, broken ties, the fragility of happiness and the cruelty of fate. This contrasts sharply with what should be a happy plot of finding true love on New Year's Eve. Just listen to this song to a poem by Bella Akhmadulina:

> For a few years now on my street
> I have heard the footsteps of my friends leaving.
> This slow departure of my friends
> Is pleasing to that darkness beyond my windows.
>
> O solitude, you are so stern!
> The iron compasses glint,
> And you close your circle so coldly
> Without listening to my useless pleas.

Do we dare to believe that on New Year's Eve fate, usually so heartless and cruel, might bring people together rather than tear them apart? Can we believe that a moment of magic can free us from the trap of this uniform life, when one is living in a uniform flat, with uniform furniture and has uniform salads on the table? Soviet uniformity is gone, but the need for New Year's magic remains. This is why we keep watching this film.

And now – a truly terrible story. A sequel to *The Irony of Fate* came out in 2007, by a different director. Even though it is filmed with the blessing of the original director, and the actors playing Zhenya and Nadya are the same, the whole premise is so awful that I would rather shut my eyes and my ears and not watch any further... there are enough disappointments in life as it is.

Language notes:

"С лёгким паром!" "Enjoy Your Bath!" or literally "[Congratulations] on the light steam!" can be said to someone who has just come out of a bath – or better still, a *banya*.

When Zhenya's friend appears on his doorstep, Zhenya's mother sends him away saying "Иди в баню!" "Go to a *banya!*" This phrase is a polite version of other expressions starting with "Иди…" "Go to…" that are usually followed by rude words. Of course, in this case *banya* is exactly where Zhenya's friend – and Zhenya himself – are about to go.

"Я понимаю, ванная в каждой квартире – это правильно, это удобно, это цивилизация, но сам процесс мытья, который в бане выглядит как торжественный обряд, в ванной – просто смывание грязи" – "I understand, to have a bathroom in every flat is right, it is convenient, it is civilization, but the process of washing, which in a *banya* seems a solemn ritual, in a bathroom is nothing more than washing off dirt" – one of Zhenya's friends turns philosophical.

"Спокойно, Ипполит, спокойно!" – "Keep calm, Ippolit, keep calm!" – When Nadya's girlfriends arrive unannounced, she presents Zhenya as her boyfriend, Ippolit, too embarrassed to say she is celebrating New Year with a man she does not know. Later on she is trying to tell the truth – but by then Zhenya has got into participating in the game and tells himself to calm down, calling himself Ippolit.

Zhenya: "Что вы меня поливаете? Я же не клумба!" – "Why are you watering me? I am not a flowerbed!" – as Nadya is pouring water on him trying to wake him up.

"Ну что вы меня всё время роняете?" – "Why do you keep dropping me?" – asks Zhenya, falling down again, as Ippolit pushes him out of the way.

"Какая гадость…" – "How disgusting…" – says Ippolit, and the viewer thinks he is referring to the presence of a strange man in his girlfriend's flat, when he continues: "… эта ваша заливная рыба" – "… your jellied fish."

"Но нашлись добрые люди: обобрали, подогрели… Нет – подобрали, обогрели" – "But there were some kind people out there – they robbed me and warmed me up… No, they picked me up and made me warm." This phrase also belongs to Ippolit, in one of his last appearances, tired and emotional. This is a play on words that is funny in Russian. "Подобрать" is to pick up, "обогреть" is to make warm. If you swap the prefixes, as Ippolit unwittingly did, "обобрать" is to rob, "подогреть" is to warm something up on a stove.

Zhenya: "Ошибки врачей дорого обходятся людям" – "Doctors' mistakes cost people dearly." Nadya: "Ошибки учителей менее заметны, но, в конечном счёте, они обходятся людям не менее дорого" – "Teachers' mistakes are less noticeable, but in the end they cost people just as dearly."

"Если у вас нет собаки,
Её не отравит сосед.
И с другом не будет драки,
Если у вас друга нет."

"If you have no dog
Your neighbour will not poison him.
And you will not have a fight with your friend,
If you have no friend."

A verse from a song called "If You Don't Have an Aunt" that Zhenya sings to Nadya, and the words of which all Russians know by heart.

"С любимыми не расставайтесь!" – this phrase, from "The Ballad of a Smoky Carriage" by little-known poet Alexander Kochetkov, became famous thanks to its being recited to music in the soundtrack of *The Irony of Fate*. The relevant verses go as follows:
"С любимыми не расставайтесь,
С любимыми не расставайтесь,
С любимыми не расставайтесь!
Всей кровью прорастайте в них.

И каждый раз навек прощайтесь,
И каждый раз навек прощайтесь,
И каждый раз навек прощайтесь
Когда уходите на миг."
"Never part with your loved ones,
Never part with your loved ones,
Never part with your loved ones,
Grow into them with your whole being.
And every time you are going away for a moment,
And every time you are going away for a moment,
And every time you are going away for a moment,
Say goodbye as if it was forever."

WHITE SUN OF THE DESERT

БЕЛОЕ СОЛНЦЕ ПУСТЫНИ

They say cosmonauts are among the most superstitious people in the world. And you too, if you have a few million to spare and would like to take off from Baikonur space station as a space tourist (following Charles Simonyi and a few others), will need to be ready to observe all the time-honoured preflight rituals, like peeing on the wheel of the bus that brings you to the launch pad, for example (if you are a woman, you are allowed to bring your urine in a jar and sprinkle it), and being sent on your journey with a friendly slap on the bottom from the flight commander. If you talk to a cosmonaut, you can never use the word "last" in the same sentence as the word "flight". And the night before the flight, tradition has it that you must watch the film *White Sun of the Desert*.

First shown in 1969, *White Sun of the Desert* is set towards the end of the Russian Civil War, around 1923, and follows the adventures of Red Army soldier Fyodor Sukhov, who is returning home through the desert to the east of the Caspian sea, in today's Turkmenistan. The desert is vast and empty; the sun is white and blinding. But all is not peaceful in this emptiness: the feuding locals bury each other alive in the sand, and Red Army units are chasing bands of warlords. One such warlord is Black Abdulla. Preparing to leave the country, he prefers to kill off his wives rather than see them become the property of another man – but he is interrupted in the process, and so has time to strangle only two of his 11-strong harem. Making his way through the desert, Sukhov bumps into the Red soldiers who rescued the harem, and is asked (or rather obliged) to look after the women while the soldiers chase Abdulla. He is left in the desert with the nine women, a rifle, a horse and the young soldier Petrukha. But far from being chased and caught, Abdulla has other plans…

Some Russian film critics have identified a genre of "Eastern" films, playing on the word "Western". According to them, "Easterns" are adventure movies based in the "Wild East" of the Russian Empire's Central Asian republics and usually set during the Civil War, with good guys and bad guys, enigmatic locals, a lot of shooting and sometimes, like Westerns, with a mythic tale underpinning the plot. I have to say, looking at the list of films which are meant to belong to this genre, I am not convinced it actually exists. These films, such as *A Friend to his Enemies, an Enemy to his Friends (Свой среди чужих, чужой среди своих)*, or *The Elusive Avengers (Неуловимые Мстители)* and, of course, *White Sun of the Desert*, are just too different and aimed at different audiences. While *The Elusive Avengers* is an implausible propaganda film for children, *A Friend to His Enemies, an Enemy to His Friends* is a philosophical exploration of identity as well as a film about someone whose name has been blackened and who has to conduct his own investigation to prove his innocence. Most films on the "Eastern" list are B-movies, and only one of them has cult status.

Describing the style of the movie, the film's director Vladimir Motyl has said that it combines both Russian folk-tale traditions and adventure-movie elements. "It is a cocktail of the Russian adventure folk-tale and a Western," he said; "I was naturally influenced by the best Westerns; I couldn't stop watching *Stagecoach*, *The Magnificent Seven* and *High Noon*."

When Motyl was three years old in 1930, his father was arrested and sent to the Gulag. Motyl's memories of his father stopped at the eye-level of a three-year-old boy – his father's boots, military trousers, and his belt. This was the last he saw of his father, when his mother caught up with the prisoners' train in a northern town on the way to the Solovki Islands and was allowed to say goodbye to her husband. Very soon the father perished in the camp. His wife was spared, but had to live in small towns in the Ural Mountains teaching at young offender institutions.

The only entertainment in these small towns was the travelling cinema showing films by Charlie Chaplin, as well as such Soviet classics as *Jolly Fellows (Весёлые ребята)* and *Chapayev (Чапаев)*. "I watched every screening – I lived for the cinema," said Motyl.

Early in his career, which began during Khrushchev's "thaw", Vladimir Motyl fell out of favour with Soviet cultural and ideological authorities. No film studio would give him a job, and his career seemed to have finished before it had properly begun.

But then he was offered a project by an experimental and relatively independent studio run by Grigory Chukhrai. Motyl initially refused the script of *White Sun of the Desert*, which seemed to him to be lacking in many ways, and which several other directors had been offered and had refused before him. But, being in no position to turn down a job, and with it looking as though he might never be offered another chance in the cinema, he took it on, having first secured from its two authors *carte blanche* to make changes. In the end, according to Motyl, the film was about 60 per cent improvised. Some dialogue was written immediately before shooting, and some characters were added or changed beyond recognition. For example: the magnificent Russian peasant woman Katerina Matveyevna with her red headscarf and a yoke with two buckets of water across her shoulders, Sukhov's wife back in his native village, was not in the original script. In the film, in Sukhov's moments of loneliness, her image appears before his eyes. In his mind he writes her ornate letters, calling her his "unforgettable Katerina Matveyevna". He does not elaborate much on his mission accompanying the harem, though, just mentioning that he had been ordered to "accompany a group of comrades" across the desert, and that lately he has had the luck to be "surrounded by mostly warm-hearted and delicate people".

Another character completely changed from the original script is Vereshchagin. Motyl wrote his lines immediately before each day's shooting.

Vereshchagin, formerly a customs officer, used to have great authority in the area, the outskirts of the Russian empire. The Civil War has brought everything into disarray, there is no power and no customs. Vereshchagin now spends his days drinking heavily and wishing his wife could get something else to eat apart from caviar (we are on the Caspian shore, and caviar is abundant, while bread is scarce). "I cannot eat this damn stuff anymore!" he complains in a famous scene, taking a spoon and staring into a big bowl of the black gold.

Vereshchagin has swapped his military uniform for a pair of peacocks that wander about the garden of his spacious house. He does not take sides in the Civil War, but drinks and suffers, watching the chaos around him. "Вот так держал!" – "This is how I held them!" – he makes a clenching movement with his fist, showing the authority he had over the region in his time.

The other thing Vereshchagin does apart from drinking is singing, accompanying himself on a guitar. The song *Your Honour, Lady Luck (Ваше благородие, госпожа Удача)* to words by Bulat Okudzhava, has become a classic. "Девять граммов в сердце постой, не зови – Не везёт мне в смерти, повезёт в любви" – "Hold on, do not ask for nine grams of lead in the heart – I have been unlucky in death, so will be lucky in love."

What is attractive in Vereshchagin is his strength, his independence and his passive resistance. The Whites, the Reds, Abdulla – he doesn't seem to care. Besides, he has promised his wife he will keep away from the conflict. But in his house he is still master, and the White officer who shouts at him promptly ends up falling out of the window. And when the time does finally come to take sides, he suddenly stands up, full of his former strength and pride.

When the film was ready, it was rejected by both cinematographic and ideological authorities, and would never have seen the light of day had Brezhnev not watched it at his *dacha* and thought it brilliant, thus giving it a green light.

The public agreed with Brezhnev. They liked the romanticism of the film, and the combination of action movie with comic touches and historic drama.

The film is set during the Civil War, but it does not by any stretch of the imagination belong to the "Civil War movie" genre, as it is not a propaganda movie, like, for example, *Chapayev*. I would not say it is a very Soviet film at all. It is not about good Reds and bad Whites, even though the Reds in the film are good, and the Whites are bad. But their ideological allegiance is not really the point.

Sukhov's attitude to life and his notion of good and bad and of his duties is much more Stoic than Soviet. When he sees a man dug into the sand, he does not hesitate to stop to help him out, even though he remarks that on the previous occasion he did so, the guy turned out to be a bandit who tried to kill him. His approach is much more to observe, to understand and to let things be than the Soviet approach of breaking, changing and rebuilding. "Восток – дело тонкое" – "The East is a delicate thing," he says, another phrase that came into common use.

It is really a fable of the journey through life, set against the abstract setting of the desert through which Sukhov makes his way, alone but confident about where he is going.

The villain Abdulla is also a bit of a philosopher. He is not just a baddie and a bandit, but represents a different, self-centred philosophical take on things: "Who in this world knows what is good and what is bad? My father said before he died: I am dying a poor man, but I hope God sends you a luxurious robe and a beautiful bridle for your horse. I waited for a long time. And then God said: go and take it all yourself, if you are brave and strong."

Director Vladimir Motyl was a child of the era when Soviet history was being rewritten. *White Sun of the Desert* was his revisionist, non-Soviet view of the Civil War, and also of the relationship of Russia with Central Asia. The Russian Empire had expanded into Central Asia during the nineteenth century. The Bolsheviks criticized the tsar's expansion, but after the October revolution quickly incorporated the non-Russian parts of the former empire into the new Soviet Union, crushing all independence movements along the way.

Officially the Soviet republics – Georgia, Ukraine, Turkmenistan, etc. – were equal members of the Soviet family. But Russia always remained the big brother, and Soviet Russians inherited from their imperial predecessors the arrogant and sometimes contemptuous attitude to their "little brothers". For the Russians of the 1970s and 1980s Central Asia (comprising the five republics Uzbekistan, Kazakhstan, Turkmenistan, Kirgizstan and Tajikistan) was the back of beyond of the Soviet state: useful, but backward, incomprehensible and scary. They could well imagine locals still burying each other in the sand for no good reason. Russians were aware that all through the Soviet time, while the big cities of the *stans* were modern and Soviet, in the isolated desert and mountain villages, traditional life and culture continued, governed by *sharia*, as well as Soviet, law. These customs sometimes included having more than one wife, although even before the revolution it would be very unusual, if not impossible, for a man to have quite as many wives as Black Abdulla – the *sharia* allowed a maximum of four.

The hidden question in the film is: what are Red Army soldiers doing in the desert, and should they be there? Sukhov has given up trying to understand the East. He is tired of fighting for world revolution in the desert. He wants to be at home, with his wife, and the film hints that this is probably the best place for him to be.

The actor who played Black Abdulla, Kakhi Kavsadze, is a Georgian actor living and working in Tbilisi. Possibly influenced by the deterioration of Russia's relationship with Georgia in recent years (Russia and Georgia went to war in 2008), he says his character is right to fight against Russians' intrusion into his land: "There was a person who lived his own life, obeyed his laws, his canons, his traditions, and suddenly someone comes and says: you have to live my way. He didn't like it. He is not a bandit, he is a person who is defending his traditions and his house. It was not he who intruded into Sukhov's house to ask him why he was sitting drinking tea from a samovar, was it?"

In the uncut version of the film Abdulla's wives weep over his body. I can imagine what impression this ending would have made: of the pointlessness of trying to change "the East – a delicate thing", of breaking traditions one does not understand.

As if it was not enough for the director to break so many of the orthodoxies of the Civil War movie, the public defiantly decided to cheer for the apolitical former customs officer Vereshchagin, who many people in the Soviet Union could immediately identify with, rather than the Red Army soldier Sukhov. Forgotten heroes, super-fluous men, great-people-turned-alcoholics, people who once saw sense in what they were doing but no longer, were plentiful in the "Era of Stagnation".

Soviet ideology was built around demanding from an ordinary person a life of self-denial and sacrifice for the motherland and the common cause. The picture of Pavlik Morozov, a young village boy who denounced his own father as a "*kulak*" (a rich peasant who exploits other peasants and hides grain from the government), dying heroically in the process, adorned the walls of every Soviet school. The other portraits on the wall were of young guerrilla fighters who died in the Second World War, sometimes after being tortured by the Nazis but never betraying their comrades. Compared to theirs, our own lives seemed insignificant and uneventful, although I have to say I was quite pleased not to have to denounce my parents to the state.

But around us we saw a society ridden with hypocrisy, where everything worked on the basis of "*blat*" – connections to those in power or those who had access to goods. Social mobility was very limited; if you were a diplomat's son or daughter you would probably become a diplomat yourself, while if your parents happened to be factory workers, you could hope at the most to become an engineer.

During the 1970s and early 1980s, the so-called "Era of Stagnation", there was a real sense, particularly among young people, of the impossibility of doing anything worthwhile. There was a huge discrepancy between an ideology that said life was useless unless one committed some extraordinary heroic deed, and the bleak reality around us, so full of restrictions (on travelling, information, etc.)

and with such limited social mobility.

All through the terrible years of Stalin's repression and the Second World War, the country nevertheless lived with a certain sense of unity, and in the belief that the sacrifice was necessary to build a new and beautiful society. Khrushchev's short-lived "thaw" brought new hope that the country would become more liberal; with the arrival of Brezhnev there came a long period of hangover and depression.

The attraction of *White Sun of the Desert* is precisely that it is different from heroic Soviet movies. Sukhov is a reluctant hero, someone who feels he has done enough, and what he would really like now is peace and quiet, just like many Soviet people at the time.

Vereshchagin, with his passive resistance, his refusal to participate in the ideological battle and his preference for a bottle of vodka and a guitar, was close to the hearts of many people. So was the sudden awakening of his pride, the great man shaking off all his fetters and rising up when someone touched him where it hurt.

During the time of *perestroika* (and even today) people also quoted his famous phrase: "I feel bad for the great State", referring to the collapse of the Soviet Union.

White Sun of the Desert is also a tale about a resourceful soldier, the famous character in the Russian fairy tale who could make porridge out of an axe. Sukhov, neat and collected, with his beard, his kettle full of water, his calm, his grin, his ability to fight alone against many using his head and not just his hands, is that quintessential Russian image of a real man of the people, a proper "*muzhik*".

This film also has something of the flavour of a medieval ballad, where Sukhov is a knight errant returning home after a long period of travelling and performing heroic deeds, who is given an undertaking he does not seek, and faces one last temptation that he heroically overcomes. He is Odysseus returning home – only how much longer will it take for him to get there, whatever happened to his wife during all this time, and will at least his dog still be alive to recognize him?

But then it is also an action film, where all the events happen in one day and the challenge is to survive it.

White Sun of the Desert is full of attractive details that give it dramatic value and deepen the plot. Sukhov's letters to his wife; his chuckle after Vereshchagin mentions that he has swapped his military coat for a couple of peacocks; his chivalry towards the women, and his devotion to his wife back home; the three enigmatic old men, unperturbed by all the shooting and explosions around them; the old photographs on Vereshchagin's wall…

The only award the film ever received was in 1998, nearly 30 years after it came out, when its creators were awarded the Russian Federation State Prize in Literature and the Arts. Until his death in February 2010, Vladimir Motyl lived in a modest apartment outside Moscow, making his living teaching young film directors how to make movies.

Meanwhile, a theme *White Sun of the Desert* restaurant now exists in Moscow, where you are greeted at the door by Vereshchagin, your order is taken by Sukhov and your food brought to you by pretty Gulchatai.

Language notes:

"Восток – дело тонкое" – "The East is a delicate thing" – a phrase used by Sukhov. It is quoted all the time, usually, but not necessarily, in relation to the East.

"Гюльчатай, открой личико!" – "Gulchatai, show your sweet face!" – the young Red soldier Petrukha falls in love with Gulchatai, even though he has never seen her face. He is trying to convince her to let him see her face, just to make sure. This phrase is used in all sorts of contexts. You can say it to ask for the true identity of someone in an internet chat room, or to comment on the French law forbidding the wearing of the burka in public institutions, or asking a girl to tell you more about herself.

"Мне за державу обидно" – "I feel bad for the great State" – Vereshchagin's phrase has been used a lot, particularly in the context of the collapse of the Soviet Union and the disintegration of Soviet institutions. "Derzhava" itself is a word without translation – it is a word for "state", but unlike the more neutral "gosudarstvo" it suggests a "great state". Being ashamed of what is going on in Russia, being under the impression that Russia is being abused by the West, Russians use this phrase, and everyone knows where it comes from. General Alexander Lebed, a prominent political figure in the 1990s, first Yeltsin's rival at the presidential elections and then his vital supporter, invoked this phrase as the title for his book *Za Derzhavu Obidno*.

"Стреляли" – "There was shooting" – At the beginning of the film, Sukhov finds a man buried in the sand as a punishment from an enemy clan. Sukhov releases him and gives him a drink of water. Later on, whenever a fight breaks out and the situation gets critical, the laconic desert man appears to help. To Sukhov's question: "Ты как здесь оказался?" – "How did you come to be here?", the man answers simply: "Стреляли..." – "There was shooting". The comic effect is achieved by the repetition, and the brevity of the phrase in Russian.

Sukhov's favourite expressions are "Это точно" – "For sure" (alternated with "Это врядли" – "this – I don't think so") and "Вопросы есть? Вопросов нет" – "Any questions? No questions."

"Одна жена любит, одна– одежду шьёт, одна – пищу варит, одна – детей кормит, и всё одна?... Тяжело!" – The harem think of Sukhov as their new master and husband. He tries to explain to the youngest of them, the pretty and curious Gulchatai, that this is not possible, as he already has a wife, and no, it is not as simple as telling her he has decided to take on a few more. Where he is from, he says, a man is only allowed to have one wife. She starts to count on her fingers: "One wife loves, one sews clothes, one cooks, one feeds the children... All this – just one wife? This is hard!" Sukhov agrees it is hard, and for a moment in his mind he has a vision of himself back in his Russian village, surrounded by the harem, each of the wives doing various chores while he is lying on a lawn drinking tea from a samovar, embracing his favourite wife, the "unforgettable Katerina Matveyevna".

Vladimir Vysotsky

Владимир Высоцкий

Russians remember the summer of 1980 for the Olympic Games held that year in Moscow. The games were boycotted by more than 50 countries because of the Soviet invasion of Afghanistan a year earlier, but this did not dampen the celebratory mood in the Soviet capital. After all, during the Cold War such "provocations" on the part of capitalist countries were to be expected.

What did cast a shadow on many people's mood was another event that happened while the games were in full swing, on 25 July 1980. This event was not officially announced, apart from a small obituary in just one newspaper and a notice on a door of the Taganka theatre cancelling that week's performance of *Hamlet*. Nevertheless, the news spread at the speed of light. On 28 July, the day of the funeral, tens of thousands of people lined the streets all around the theatre. They had come to say their goodbyes to Vladimir Vysotsky, a singer-songwriter and actor who felt like a member of the family.

Vysotsky was born in Moscow in 1938. He became a household name in the USSR mainly for his songs, poems set to music that he sang accompanying himself on a Russian seven-stringed guitar. He also gained public acclaim as an actor at the avant-garde Taganka theatre and for his roles in several films. Despite all attempts by the Soviet authorities to suppress the distribution of his work, he gained almost mythical status during his life.

Vysotsky came from a family of Soviet intelligentsia – his father was a military man, his mother a translator of German books. Although this sounds like a perfectly middle-class family to be born into, the conditions in late 1930s Moscow were far from middle class. His childhood was famously (because of his song "The Ballad of Childhood" – "Баллада о детстве") spent with his family in a room in a communal flat, where, if you believe the song, the occupants of the 38 rooms all had to share one bathroom.

His own attempt to become a regular Soviet engineer was short-lived. He abandoned the engineering course in the middle of his first year to enrol at acting school. A couple of years after graduation, he joined the brand-new Taganka theatre, and became the centre of its legendary 1960s–1970s period under the director Yuri Lubimov.

It is hard to imagine in this age of information overload the importance that this theatre had. Classical plays were reinterpreted and dealt obliquely with contemporary issues – like, for example, the *Hamlet* premiered in 1971 starring Vysotsky, in which the hero was a modern intellectual trying to find his way between various ethical choices, fighting alone against the state machine.

Another play staged by Lubimov at Taganka was *The Life of Galileo* by Bertolt Brecht. The scientist has been threatened with torture by the church authorities and renounces his scientific convictions. The play, also with Vysotsky, explored a public figure's right to compromise with an oppressive regime, and a scientist's responsibility to his work.

These shows were subversive in their content, and in their form they broke away from classical theatre traditions (the actors played more than one role and would go among the audience in the intervals, performing in modern clothes). People were prepared to queue for hours at any time of day or night to get tickets.

Vysotsky was the biggest star at the Taganka theatre, and he also starred in several films. But it is for his songs that he is best loved and remembered.

From his teenage years Vysotsky had been writing songs and playing them to his friends. His early ballads were inspired by the Moscow yards – *dvory* – and the semi-delinquent activities of the youth who populated them. This was how war-children lived, many of whom had lost their fathers either in the war or in Stalin's purges. Their mothers were working hard and did not have much time to spend on their children's upbringing. So the children ran wild – "we grew like grass", I once heard someone say about those times. With the war over and glorified the boys wished they had been old enough to participate. Weapons were all around and easily available ("The snot-nosed criminals were making some fine deals: at a building site, the captive Germans were happy to exchange knives for bread," wrote Vysotsky in "The Ballad of Childhood"). "Innocent" street confrontations led to street gangs, and many of those boys ended up being seduced by the romance of criminal life.

But even good boys and girls liked to listen to these hard-bitten songs. These usually evoked a tough man in sensitive mode. Vysotsky tapped into the genre in his early creative years, writing songs like "The One Who Used to Be with Her": "That evening I didn't drink or sing, I just gazed at her like a child. But the one who used to be with her told me I should go, that there was nothing for me there"; "one day in the autumn I was walking with a friend and we saw them standing waiting silently in a row, eight of them."

Vysotsky also tapped into the prison-folklore genre, which in the USSR was not quite the same as criminal folklore, since most people who wound up in prison weren't criminals. During Stalin's time the population of the Gulag numbered around two and a half million people, so we can guess that a lot of prison songs were written by purge victims.

It is not clear which of the two, a criminal or a Gulag prisoner, is the character in Vysotsky's song "Hey, Driver!" ("Эй, шофёр!") who asks the taxi to take him on a nostalgic tour around some of Moscow's old prisons, only to find out that they have been closed down or demolished. He invites the driver to drink to "no more prisons or camps in Russia".

"The Bathouse" ("Банька"), a song written a while later, is about someone who has spent a long time in the Gulag and has been released after Stalin's death. On his way home he stops at a peasant house and asks the hostess to prepare him a banya so he can wash away not only the dirt, but also the memories of his ordeal:

"So much faith and so many trees have tumbled down,
So much misfortune and so many railway routes explored
On my left breast there is the profile of Stalin
On my right breast Marinka full face.
…

And later in pits or in the marshes
Swallowing tears and rotgut
We were tattooing his profile closer to our hearts
So that he could hear hearts tearing apart."

Russian prison tattoos are a topic in their own right; many prisoners tattooed Stalin's profile over their heart, in the (vain) hope that the guards would not shoot at his picture.

Vysotsky's later songs were about the absurdities of Soviet life, the desperation of down-and-out alcoholics, friendship and betrayal, the war, funny stories from the life of sportsmen, dysfunctional families, love, life and death.

Vysotsky's range of topics was limitless. He would transform himself from an alcoholic ("if you reckon it our way we did not drink so much, I swear I am not lying – tell them, Seryoga!") into a peasant lost in the capital, into a delinquent, a soldier in the trenches, even into a microphone or a fighter plane. Being an actor, he tended to perform his songs as though they were theatrical vignettes, with a hero and sometimes dialogue.

His satirical songs are pretty mild. On unfair privileges: "People kept muttering, people wanted justice: we were first in the queue, and those who came later are already eating!" On hypocrisy when meeting foreigners: "If they start debates with vodka, tell them: no, democrat lads, only tea! Reject their presents – show them we have more than enough of this stuff at home!"

Even though not openly dissident, Vysotsky had one theme that ran through his songs and which was very much out of line with the Soviet hierarchical ideology: the importance of making moral choices and sticking to them even when you are one against all. This theme is most obvious in his song "The one who did not shoot" ("Тот, который не стрелял"), about an anonymous member of a platoon refusing to take part in the execution of his fellow-soldier. What interested Vysotsky was people's behaviour in extreme circumstances, either in the war, in the mountains or between two drivers inside the cabin of a long distance truck breaking down in a snowstorm in the middle of nowhere: "I told him: 'stop whining', but he reached for a spanner, giving me that wolf-like look – he could be rough. And I realized around us were 500 kilometres of wilderness, and the one who outlives the other will prove he was in the right."

An individualistic or anarchic attitude is fairly typical for singer-songwriters all over the world. You cannot really call Vysotsky individualistic. He really wants to belong to "the people". He is fervently patriotic. He usually does not want to destroy social structures (although he sometimes ponders how nice it would be to "lie at the bottom of the sea, like a submarine" or to leave everything behind and go to Magadan, a place in Siberia so remote no one but prisoners ever goes there). In Vysotsky's case the individualism is all about personal responsibility and making ethical choices. His soldier who refuses to shoot is different from Boris Vian's "Le déserteur" – he is not someone who withdraws in disappointment at the way the world works, but stays within the structure and makes a moral decision despite the consequences.

Like his counterparts in the West, Vysotsky drew on folk melodies, including Russian gypsy tunes. He accompanied himself on a Russian seven-string guitar, which he liked to tune a tone and a half down. Pretty much all of his songs are written in minor key, the earlier ones in C and the later ones in A minor. The combination of the minor key and the repetitive folk melodies that one friend has characterized as "relentless", relay that very Russian sensation of doom, this untranslatable *toska*, the mixture of longing, yearning, desperation and depression.

And then there is the singer's unique voice, a mix of the rasping seductiveness of Serge Gainsbourg, the earnestness of Johnny Cash and Tom Waits' gravelly growl, intensified by Vysotsky's habit of prolonging consonants, particularly the rolling Russian "rrr".

Vysotsky was only one of the singer-songwriters of the period, one of the *bards*, as they came to be known. His songs are not as subtle poetically as those of Bulat Okudzhava, nor are they as radical as some others. Yuly Kim, for example wrote much more bitter songs and was part of the dissident movement. The wrath of the Soviet government at Alexander Galich's take on Russia's present and history forced him to emigrate.

But it was Vysotsky who became universally loved. Perhaps it was his ability to get into the skin of another person; perhaps it is precisely because he was more mainstream than the others. He was also more engaging and more intense. He was not too much of an intellectual, he was a *хороший мужик*, the best thing you can say about a man in Russia, roughly as "a good bloke". "*Muzhik*" means peasant, so "*khoroshy muzhik*" is a bloke who is down to earth, has common roots, knows how to drink, can be relied on, is not a wimp.

But Vysotsky did defy officialdom – not because his songs were about politics but just by describing life exactly as it was. For the Soviet people, so used to living in a schizophrenic situation where the official version of life in the USSR had nothing to do with their real life, to hear someone saying how things really were was a breath of fresh air.

Vysotsky became an unofficial legend, never seen on TV (except in a few films) or heard on the radio. Having written around 600 songs, he famously had almost no official recordings issued during his lifetime. He did perform when he had a chance – at workers' cultural centres, village clubs and private apartments. His performances were secretly recorded and copied from one tape recorder to another, until his voice, so hoarse and mesmerizing, would be changed almost beyond recognition.

Looking at it from a Western point of view, it seems impossible and absurd that someone can become a huge popular star but be completely ignored by the press, have hardly any of his songs released and be denied official concerts. His admirers had only a vague idea what their idol looked like or how old he was and fed on rumours about his biography and personal life. If you were lucky enough to get tickets, you could see him perform at the Taganka, or hear him singing at rare semi-official concerts. "Recognizing" the characters in his songs as people they used to know, listeners would write asking whether he was that very Volodya they shared a trench with in 1943 (Vysotsky was born in 1938, so he was much too young for that) or a prison cell (though his knowledge of the world of the delinquents was purely second-hand).

What Vysotsky wrote from first-hand experience were songs about alcoholics. The singer's health had started to cave in early on because of his Russian-style alcohol abuse. I heard the English chef and reformed alcoholic Clarissa Dickson-Wright's story about how she was asked by her doctor if she had ever been treated for malaria, because her blood seemed similar to that of people who had been dosed with quinine, and she realized it came from the years when she was really knocking back the gin and tonic. Without diminishing the seriousness of her alcoholism or the triumph of her recovery, my first thought was that I could not imagine a Russian alcoholic ever bothering with tonic. Nor with gin, for that matter. Vodka, the bootleg rotgut (*samogon*), cheap eau de cologne or industrial alcohol-containing liquids were more the thing.

In 1969 Vysotsky was so nearly dead after a binge that the paramedics refused to take him to hospital so as not to spoil their team's death-in-transportation record. It was only the insistence of his French wife Marina Vlady that saved his life.

In 1979 Vysotsky experienced clinical death on exactly the same date on which he died in 1980, at the age of 42. After his death Marina wrote a book, *Vladimir, ou le vol arrêté – Vladimir, or the Aborted Flight.* When the book was translated from French and published in Russia, the graphic depiction of the bard's addiction problems and her comments on his family shocked Russians who weren't used to this tell-all biographical style. "De mortuis aut bene aut nihil" – "Speak well of the dead or not at all" is the prevalent attitude in Russia, and you are particularly not supposed to talk so candidly about such a beloved figure as Vladimir Vysotsky.

But Marina Vlady was Vysotsky's guardian angel for the last 12 years of his life, sometimes interrupting filming in France to fly urgently to Moscow to get him out of a drinking binge. Meanwhile, the singer described his own attitude in his song "Capricious Horses", in which he lashes the horses that are taking him to his "last refuge", hurrying them on, at the same time begging them to go just a little bit more slowly.

A few more words should be said about Marina Vlady, Vysotsky's last wife, a French actress of Russian descent. The whole of Russia was in love with Marina Vlady after her film *The Sorceress* (1955), based on a story by the Russian writer Alexander Kuprin. A member of the French communist party, she often travelled to Russian film festivals. She spoke beautiful, old-fashioned Russian with just a hint of a charming foreign accent.

When in 1967 Marina came to the Moscow film festival, her friends took her to the Taganka to see an avant-garde production. Later that evening she met the troupe. The moment he arrived, Vysotsky told Marina he had been in love with her ever since he had first seen her on screen and that he meant to marry her.

Coming to Moscow a few months later with her three children, and sending them to a Young Pioneer (scout) camp to learn Russian, Marina was amused when they sang her a song they learnt from their Russian fellow scouts. A working-class family couple is preparing to go out:

Do we really have to get all dressed up?
Tell me honey, for Christ's sake!
She answers: Get dressed, I'm ashamed of you!
Or you'll have to walk a few steps behind, as usual.

She says: I borrowed a dress from Nadya,
Today I will be just like Marina Vlady.
And whatever it costs me, I will spend my Sunday
Dressed up, even with your drunken face.

Marina Vlady was very amused, particularly when she found out who the author was.

She took Vysotsky to see the world, although it was not easy to get him permission to travel outside the Soviet Union. The first place they visited happened to be West Berlin. Vysotsky started vomiting when he saw the shop windows full of sausages, meat and fruit; having been brought up with the war a recent memory, he could not believe this was how the losing side lived. "But they lost the war, and they have everything!" he said. "We won, and we have nothing!"

What makes Vysotsky a presence in today's Russia? For my generation he is a kind of paternal figure, maybe because so many of our fathers performed his songs in the kitchen, accompanying themselves with three chords on the guitar. In a divided Russian society, Vysotsky is someone who is easy to like, and maybe he fits that dream of some honest, strong character around whom feuding groups can unite.

Lastly, it is worth mentioning that in December 2011 the film *Vysotsky: Thanks for Being Alive (Высоцкий. Спасибо, что живой)* came out. An unusual thing about this film was that the actor who played the main role was to be left anonymous, even to his fellow actors (he came to the filming already heavily disguised). A silicon "robot" face was used to achieve an extraordinary resemblance to the bard. Nikita Vysotsky, son of the singer (from an earlier marriage) who wrote the script, said they did not want to reveal the actor's identity, since they wanted to create the image of Vysotsky without another person standing in the way. The film was received with great hostility by most cinema critics and by Marina Vlady, who all declared it was devoid of content and relied exclusively on the sensationalism of this "cinematic cloning".

Language notes:

Все жили вровень, скромно так –
Система коридорная:
На тридцать восемь комнаток
Всего одна уборная.
Здесь на́ зуб зуб не попадал,
Не грела телогреечка.
Здесь я доподлинно узнал
Почём она, копеечка.

Everyone lived equally modestly,
There was a "corridor system":
For the thirty eight-bedrooms
There was only one bathroom.
The cold made your teeth chatter
And a padded coat did not warm you
Here I truly found out
The price of a kopek.

(from "Баллада о детстве" – "The Ballad of Childhood")

Вели дела отменные
Сопливые острожники:
На стройке немцы пленные
На хлеб меняли ножики

The snot-nosed criminals
Were making fine deals
At a building site, the captive Germans
Were happy to exchange knives for bread

(from "Баллада о детстве" – "The Ballad of Childhood")

В тот вечер я не пил, не пел,
Я на неё вовсю глядел,
Как смотрят дети,
Как смотрят дети.
Но тот, кто раньше с нею был,
Сказал мне, чтоб я уходил,
Сказал мне, чтоб я уходил,
Что мне не светит.

That evening I didn't drink or sing,
I just gazed at her like a child.
But the one who used to be with her
Told me I should go,
That there was nothing for me there.

(from "Тот, что раньше с нею был" – "The One Who Used to Be with Her")

Будут с водкою дебаты, отвечай:
Нет, ребята-демократы, только чай!
От подарков их сурово отвернись:
Мол, у самих добра такого – завались.

If they start debates with vodka, tell them:
no, democrat lads, only tea!
Reject their presents –
show them we have more than enough of this stuff at home!

(from "Инструкция перед поездкой за рубеж" – "Instructions
Before a Trip Abroad")

Мы в очереди первыми стояли,
А те, кто сзади нас, уже едят!

We were first in the queue,
and those who came later are already eating!

(from "А люди всё роптали и роптали" – "People Kept Muttering")

Чуть помедленнее, кони,
Чуть помедленнее!
Вы тугую не слушайте плеть.
Но что-то кони мне попались
Привередливые...
И дожить не успел,
Мне допеть не успеть...

A bit slower, horses,
A bit slower!
Do not listen to the cracking lash.
But I seem to have
Some capricious horses...
I have not had time to finish living,
I will not have time to finish singing...

(from "Кони привередливые" – "Capricious Horses")

The twelve chairs

Двенадцать стульев

What are they like, today's young Russians? Having left Moscow in 1996, do I really know who they are, what they like, what makes them laugh or cry? As someone who grew up in the USSR, I feel I have more in common with Russians ten, twenty, even thirty years older than me than with these young creatures who have never known anything but capitalism *à la russe*. I read twentysomething Russians' messages on internet forums and shake my head in disapproval at the randomness of their spelling and punctuation. One stereotype of Russians in the West is that they are great readers, but reading books does not seem to be these young Russians' favourite pastime. Still, it is comforting and amusing to see that *The Twelve Chairs (Двенадцать стульев)* crops up in the list of those books that they do read and enjoy.

There are at least three reasons why this satirical novel first published in 1928 is still read now. First, so many phrases from it entered everyday use that young Russians, when they start reading the book, immediately recognize the linguistic world they are entering. Secondly, because in capitalist Russia this book, its subject matter (a treasure hunt) and its characters (a professional conman, among others) have acquired a new life, and a new reading. The third reason is that to Russian readers this book is simply, and timelessly, funny.

The Twelve Chairs was written in 1927 by Ilya Ilf and Yevgeny Petrov, comic writers from Odessa. It is set in that same year.

The hero of this satire is Ostap Bender, a resourceful young crook with a murky past, no socks on his feet but hundreds of ideas in his head.

By a quirk of fate he meets an old aristocrat, Ippolit Matveyevich Vorobyaninov, who has just been told by his dying mother-in-law that she sewed all her diamonds into the upholstery of one of the family's set of dining chairs. But the chairs have been scattered about the country, and the pair have to run the length and breadth of the young Union of Soviet Socialist Republics to find the one that houses the treasure.

Ostap and Vorobyaninov meet many people and find out a lot of things about life in the USSR in the mid-1920s during their search for the chairs. They encounter apathetic inhabitants of provincial towns, businessmen sympathizers of the pre-revolutionary regime, drunk and confused caretakers, naive chess-lovers and a young, female dedicated follower of fashion (Ellochka the Cannibal) who gets by happily with a vocabulary of only 30 words.

They sleep in overcrowded student dormitories full of squatters, go along the Volga on a propaganda boat, and in the Caucasus mountains dance a Caucasian folk dance, competing with the local kids for a few coins from the tourists.

Will they ever find the treasure? Right to the very end, the book keeps you guessing.

The history of the novel's creation is interesting. It involves not only the two authors, Ilya Ilf (real name Fainzilberg) and Yevgeny Petrov (real name Katayev), but also Petrov's elder brother, Valentin Katayev, himself a brilliant writer who helped several generations of young writers and poets, and somehow managed to stay at peace with the state and live to be almost 90.

Katayev the elder was the first to leave his native Odessa, a multicultural, lively city on the Black Sea, setting off on a mission to conquer the capital.

Katayev's friend Ilya Fainzilberg and younger brother Yevgeny Katayev swiftly followed. Arriving in Moscow, all three started to work for a railway workers' trade union publication with the not very poetic name *The Whistle (Гудок)*. This does not sound like any ambitious young journalist's dream, but in those years it was precisely that. In the 1920s this newspaper had gathered together many talented authors, including Mikhail Bulgakov and Yuri Olesha. They were mostly writing comic and satirical stories. The 1920s was the golden age of satire in Soviet Russia; this was in a sense a product of Lenin's New Economic Policy, of which more later.

It was Valentin Katayev's idea that his younger brother and Ilya Fainzilberg (who knew each other but were not particularly close friends) should try writing together. He also came up with the treasure-chase plot. He initially planned to use the pair as his collaborators and publish the book under his own name (by then, Valentin had become a successful writer, and had more literary magazines and publishers willing to publish his work than he had time to write).

But as soon as the pair presented the chapters they had written so far, Katayev realised that he was not needed any more, as the novel had acquired a life of its own under his little brother's and his friend's combined pen. Katayev renounced the authorship of the novel, and gave it over entirely to the pair's hands.

And so in 1928 this classic of satirical prose was published, under the pen-names of Ilya Ilf and Yevegy Petrov. This was also the beginning of the writers' creative tandem that lasted for 10 years until Ilf's death. They are forever yoked together as Ilf-and-Petrov,

How did they write together? Not without difficulty, it seems. They once wrote in a preface to their book: "We are not relatives. Not even the same age. And of different ethnicity: while one of us is a Russian (a mysterious Slavic soul) the other one is a Jew (a mysterious Jewish soul). So, it is hard to work together. The most difficult thing is to achieve that harmonious moment when both authors can finally sit down at the desk. While one of the authors is full of creative energy the other one (oh, the mysterious Slavic soul!) is lying on the sofa, feet up, reading the history of sea battles. At the same time he announces that he is seriously (most probably mortally) ill.

Or it can also be the other way round. The Slavic soul suddenly gets up from the sickbed, and says that he has never felt so inspired in his life. But the other author (oh, the mysterious Jewish soul!) does not want to, cannot work. You see, right now he has no inspiration. And in fact, he is thinking of going away to the Far East to broaden his horizons… It is quite impossible to see how we can write together."

Nobody knows for sure how Ilf and Petrov thought up the charismatic figure of Ostap Bender, the young eloquent crook tireless in his resourcefulness and somehow doomed to failure, a quintessentially negative character who nevertheless arouses our sympathy. Some sources even name Katayev the elder as a prototype, but many think the character combined features of several of the creators' friends.

To better understand this novel, it is worth reminding ourselves of the era in which it was written.

Imagine Russia in the late 1920s. World War I, which shook the foundations of the Russian monarchy, is over. The bourgeois revolution of February 1917 got rid of the tsar, but the new government was in turn turfed out by the Bolshevik takeover in October the same year. The civil war that followed lasted until 1922 and left the country in ruins. The terrible famine of 1921-1923, resulting from the Bolshevik policy of expropriating grain from the peasants, together with an unusually severe drought, affected practically the whole of the country, but was particularly severe in the Volga region, the South Urals and Ukraine.

In 1921, seeing that the policy of 'military communism' was leading the country to the verge of collapse, and pressed by numerous uprisings of peasants, workers and the navy, who demanded a parliament "without communists", Lenin resorted to re-introducing an economic system he knew to work – capitalism. Private property and commerce were once again permitted. The tax burden on peasants was massively reduced. Foreign investments were lured into Soviet Russia, now that you could once again do business. This was called the New Economic Policy, and is known by the abbreviation of NEP. It existed until the early 1930s, when Stalin put an end to it.

NEP seemed like a complete U-turn for Bolshevik revolutionary ideology – the releasing of the "market devil", as Leon Trotsky called it. What only a couple of years before had been not only frowned upon, but extremely dangerous (conducting commercial operations, opening a business, owning property, gambling, etc.) suddenly became possible again. Casinos opened their doors, Moscow coachmen once again offered to take the well-to-do to the fashionable out-of-town restaurant Yar. Once again, it became fashionable to take cocaine, drink Madeira and show off your wealth. While this was the case in Moscow, in some rural areas the villagers continued to die of starvation. But in the big cities, after the years of war, hunger and upheavals, NEP offered a sudden glimpse of stability and the hope that life was going back to the way people knew it. Not just to pre-revolutionary times, but to the time before the First World War, which many people saw as giving rise to a long period of calamity.

As most of the old bourgeoisie had emigrated or been killed during the revolution, the fortunes that were made during NEP belonged to *nouveaux riches* similar in their tastes to those who appeared after the collapse of the Soviet Union in the 1990s.

A NEPman was not a member of the pre-revolutionary bourgeois elite. The *sovbur* (*советский буржуй*, the Soviet bourgeois) who appeared during NEP had low social origins. Reading the literature and memoirs of the time, you can imagine them: former couriers, peasants and cobblers, as well as professional criminals, walking around dressed in the latest fashion, their girlfriends showing off the jewellery that had been bartered during the previous years of hunger by aristocratic women in exchange for a chunk of bacon. And in a similar way to what happened during *perestroika* in the 1990s, party officials spied a chance to get rich.

Valentin Katayev in *My Crown of Diamonds* described his trips to a casino together with then not very well-known Mikhail Bulgakov: "Around the table stood and sat the gamblers, the scary creatures with the even more scary names: 'private owners', 'NEPmen', or 'sovburs'. Each one of them bore this special stamp of temporary, unlawful wealth, crookedness, insolence, attachment to petty-bourgeois values mixed with hidden fear. They were dressed in new well-ironed double-breasted suits... Rings shone on their chubby fingers." This was when Katayev and Bulgakov would take their last couple of roubles to a casino, and then run with their win to Yeliseyevsky's shop on Tverskaya street to buy a bottle of port and "ham, sausage, sardines, fresh bread and cheddar – always cheddar!" that Bulgakov particularly liked, while a hungry bunch of friends waited at home.

The following description of a NEPman is taken from a novel by Anatoly Mariengof, *Cynics (Циники)*:

"I am not surprised any more when today I see him wearing a sable hat and Siberian furs, and tomorrow a threadbare coat, the day after tomorrow a Red Army greatcoat, and then a sheepskin jerkin or a 1918-style commissar's leather jacket.

He changes not only his clothes, but his expression, his gestures, the look in his eyes and his gait. Dokuchaev is convinced that a man should be made more or less like a good English wash-bag that has everything necessary for a trip around the world, from a box of condoms to an icon of Our Lady. He does not understand how there can exist people with definite feelings, qualities and norms."

And this is the time in which *The Twelve Chairs* is set, the short period of wild capitalism sandwiched between the upheavals of the revolution and the brutalization of the Soviet system under Stalin.

When we first see Ostap Bender with no coat, no socks, no home and no money, but wearing chic lacquered shoes, we think: where did he come from? It is logical to suppose he must have been released from prison where, in all probability, he had ended up for petty conman-type activity.

Many episodes in the novel refer specifically to the period. For example, the 1920s saw the proliferation of street children (*беспризорники*) whose parents had been killed or died during the famine. And only during NEP, and not any other period of the USSR's history would an enterprising priest have dreamed of setting up his own candle factory.

Despite being set in a very specific moment in Soviet history, various generations of Russians in the Soviet and post-Soviet times have continued to enjoy reading the novel. So, what has made this book so enduringly popular?

Importantly, it is still funny today. Ilf and Petrov make fun of everyone – the old aristocrat, the NEPmen, Soviet students, drunken caretakers and talentless poets. Even though life in the Soviet Union and then post-Soviet Russia has constantly changed on the surface since 1927, Ilf and Petrov somehow managed to capture an unchanging essence and show the reader the funny side of their day-to-day life. In a country with such a tragic history and such a strong tradition of bureaucratic suppression of the individual, being able to stand back, to laugh at the place, is a vital survival tactic.

Ostap Bender celebrates the individualism so thoroughly suppressed during Soviet times. The figure of a lonely hero, an individualist, a cowboy who comes from nowhere and disappears into nowhere, so typical in Westerns and so alien to Soviet culture, is universally attractive, because it awakens a suppressed longing for freedom from authority. Ostap Bender, the lonely Soviet cowboy, is doubly attractive because he is the only one of his kind in Soviet-era literature, as far as I can see. He is just as attractive as the Clint Eastwood gunslinger, although he is a different type of loner – not a gloomy man of few words with no name, but a sparkling, witty, never despairing, always optimistic rascal, whose prime motive in the treasure-hunt is a childlike enthusiasm for the game more than greed.

I remember when I was reading *The Twelve Chairs* in the 1980s I had the sensation that Ostap was the only person who seemed normal in a crazy world. All around him was chaos, a disintegrated world where three clocks at a train station all showed different times, and everyone was getting lost in the newly renamed streets. The system, society itself, was crazy, while Ostap was normal, and was taking advantage of the system, trying to beat it.

His energy, which, according to Soviet norms, should have been used in some collective enterprise, is being used in an individualistic pursuit. Ostap is one against all, a person of huge energy and abilities, limited in what he can achieve by the society in which he lives, but challenging these limitations and accepting the difficulties with good humour. You can never imagine Ostap actually getting the treasure and becoming a millionaire, as his raison d'être is in the chase, in the process, and not in the result.

Ostap does not complain about society, and he certainly does not try to change it. He is a skilful seaman, who manoeuvres in the sea of human weaknesses, using them to his advantage. At the same time, he manages to do it with charm, and without oppressing others.

Ostap is an artist in need of an audience – and we, the readers, are happy to respond to this need. We feel in the novel he does not get the audience he deserves, as Ippolit is too stupid and too preoccupied with the diamond chase to appreciate his companion's artistry. Ostap Bender, with his extrovert generosity, sticks with Ippolit through the thick and thin of the treasure chase, when in fact Ippolit is nothing but a liability, and all the chairs they locate are thanks to Ostap's efforts.

Identifying yourself with Ostap raised you above Soviet reality, made you witty and enterprising, resourceful and always hopeful. It is the optimism of the book and its hero, I am sure, that makes people read it again and again. Never give up, even with no socks on your feet!

And of course, the sparkling, witty language, the turns of phrase and metaphors, which still sound fresh, make it a pleasure to read.

This novel is so supple that, while it was presented in Soviet editions as a satire on everything inimical to the Soviet way of life, now in capitalist Russia it is sometimes presented with equal glibness as an "anti-Soviet" book.

Ilf and Petrov were by no means "anti-Soviet" writers. It is clear from their biography and their other works that they were seduced by the romance of the revolution, and saw themselves very much as part of the young Soviet state.

It has been suggested that the book was a response to a certain political situation, being written during the argument between on one hand Stalin and Bukharin, who supported NEP as a necessary temporary survival measure for the Soviet State, and Trotsky on the other, who thought NEP a betrayal of world revolution. The book was meant to support Stalin's and Bukharin's point of view, that world revolution was still far off, and meanwhile the Soviet State was strong and the "market devil" and the counterrevolutionary elements were laughably weak. Petrov's elder brother Valentin Katayev had good connections among literary functionaries and politicians, and an excellent nose for the political climate. He probably suggested to the authors the political tone for the novel, and acted as a guarantor in the face of the censors. Even though the political situation changed soon after the publication of the book (Stalin had defeated Trotsky, manoeuvred Bukharin out of power, changed his mind about the NEP and wanted quick industrialization) the authors had powerful protectors among high-ranking literary functionaries (such as Vladimir Narbut and Mikhail Koltsov). Its publication also coincided with a big argument in the press about the role of satire, and whether it was necessary at all in the workers' and peasants' state. Ilf and Petrov took part in the discussion, obviously on the side of satire, and defeated their opponents. An article "On the Ways of Soviet Satire" in the *Literaturnaya Gazeta* pronounced that satire would keep denouncing prejudice, religion, nationalism, bureaucracy, philistinism and Western influences: not only was satire's right to exist sanctioned, but also its range of permissible targets.

In 1931 Ilf and Petrov published another novel, *The Golden Calf* (*Золотой телёнок*), chronicling the further adventures of Ostap Bender. In the sequel, he is as enterprising as ever in pursuing the money of a clandestine Soviet millionaire, although possibly his lust for life seems to have dimmed a bit.

The Twelve Chairs was still read and quoted by my classmates in the 1980s. In post-Soviet Russia the figure of Ostap Bender was elevated to "*предприниматель*" – entrepreneur – rather than crook, and his statue adorns several Russian towns. In his creators' native city, Odessa, there is a commemorative plaque to Bender, and a statue of a chair from the novel on one of the main streets, Deribasovskaya.

The novel has been turned into a film three times in Russia, in 1971, in 1976 and 2004; there is also a 1970 US version by Mel Brooks. Most Russians don't know there is also a classic Cuban film based on the same novel, although transferred to Cuban postrevolutionary reality. Made in 1962, only three years after the revolution, *Las doce sillas* follows the adventures of a young Oscar and Cuban landowner Don Hipólito in the new and, to them, alien Republic of Cuba.

Language notes:

"Может быть, тебе дать ещё ключ от квартиры, где деньги лежат?" – "Maybe I should also give you the key from the flat where the money is?" – the phrase belongs to Ostap Bender, and you can use it when you think someone is being cheeky in asking you too much.

"Заседание продолжается! Лёд тронулся, господа присяжные заседатели!" – "The trial continues! The ice has cracked, gentlemen of the jury!" – this is what Ostap keeps saying when he suddenly sniffs the trail of another chair.

"Запад нам поможет. Крепитесь." – "The West will help us. Be strong" – says Ostap at a meeting of a newly-created counterrevolutionary society. It can be used ironically when you want to say "nothing will help us now".

"Деньги вперёд, – заявил монтер, – утром – деньги, вечером – стулья или вечером – деньги, а на другой день утром – стулья." "Money first, – said the electrician, – money in the morning – chairs in the evening, or money in the evening – chairs the next day in the morning." This is quoted a lot when Russians want to emphasize they want money first.

"Я человек, измученный нарзаном" – "I am a person suffering from Narzan." Narzan is mineral water from the Caucasus. The electrician who is ready to sell our heroes the chairs is referring to the fact that he hasn't had a proper drink for a long time. Can be used to say: "What do you have to do to get a drink around here?"

"Дело помощи утопающим – дело рук самих утопающих" – "Saving someone from drowning is in the hands of the person who is drowning." A poster near the river. Can be used to say: "It's not our problem".

"Знойная женщина — мечта поэта" – "An ardent woman is a poet's dream" – Ostap marries an opulent widow to get away with her chair. It is used to describe a voluptuous woman.

"Же не манж па сис жю" ("Je ne mange pas six jours") – "I have not eaten for six days." Ostap and Vorobyaninov are in the Caucasus with no money, and Ostap makes the old aristocrat beg in French, pretending he is a former member of the old pre-Soviet parliament. Ippolit is outraged: "Никогда ещё Воробьянинов не протягивал руки?!" – "Vorobyaninov has never stretched out his hand!" "Так протянете ноги, старый дуралей!" – "Then you will stretch out your legs [kick the bucket], old fool!", answers Ostap.

When Ostap is inspired (or very hungry) he is unstoppable in his skill at convincing people to hand over their money. "Остапа несло" – "Ostap was carried away" is a phrase used by Ilf and Petrov, and also used by Russians in day-to-day speech to show someone is over-enthusiastic, or making unrealistic dreams, or has gone too far when lying.

"Командовать парадом буду я!" – "*I* shall command the parade!" Ostap likes to say.

Moscow does not believe in tears
Москва слезам не верит

There are many sayings about Moscow: "When you go to Moscow, take your last kopek with you" – "В Москву идти – последнюю копейку нести". "In Moscow the church bells are loud, but the dinner is small" – "В Москве толсто звонят, да тонко едят". "Moscow is a mother to some, a stepmother to others" – "Москва – кому мать, кому мачеха". You can tell those sayings came from Moscow's struggling "stepsons" and "stepdaughters". Like any big city, Moscow has always attracted people from other places, people running away from poverty, looking for a better life or trying to make it big. Another saying about Moscow the wicked stepmother claims "Moscow does not trust tears". The big city doesn't care about your despair; you'd better pull yourself together and start sorting the situation out.

Moscow Does Not Believe in Tears (Москва слезам не верит) is a film made in 1979 and loved ever since by Russians. "… trust tears" rather than "… believe in tears" would have been a more correct translation, but I will use the title this movie is known by in English.

The film opens with a song that says "Moscow was not built in a day" (Москва не сразу строилась). This is what you say to encourage someone who feels impatient and frustrated, to say: "It takes time and effort to achieve something", just like the English expression "Rome wasn't built in a day". The title and the song tell us what the film is about: building a new life in a big, uncaring city.

The movie follows the story of three young women from the provinces who have come to Moscow in search of a better life. They share a room in a workers' hostel and they are best friends, even though their personalities could not be more different.

Tonya is a nice, level-headed, homeloving country girl, who has already found herself a nice, hardworking young man. He takes her to see his parents and asks her advice on what they should plant in the family's allotment, from which we deduce that the relationship is getting serious. The second girl, Ludmilla, is a bit of a gold-digger who laughs at her friends' naivety and lack of adventure. For her, Moscow is "a big lottery", where you can suddenly win "everything, and right now!" While working at an industrial bakery, she is constantly planning how to land herself a Muscovite husband with good prospects. The third girl, Katya, is a serious student, a straight, hard-working character who gets caught up in Ludmilla's schemes, and will be the one to pay the price…

For Katya, Tonya and Ludmilla Moscow is a dream city, as it was for the three sisters in Anton Chekhov's play. But for Chekhov's sisters Moscow represents a lost paradise, and their cry: "To Moscow!" expresses their longing for change in their lives. The three girls from *Moscow Does Not Believe in Tears* are a lot more down to earth. They all know why they are striving to stay in the capital and what they want to achieve: for Tonya it is stability, for Katya a career, for Ludmilla a comfortable life with a Muscovite husband.

In the first part of the film we are in the Moscow of 1958: the girls wear dresses with tight-fitting tops, flowing skirts and white socks. The community guards with red armbands stop and shame a couple for embracing in public. Five years have passed since Stalin's death. To make the point that this is the beginning of a new and freer era, we see a poet performing on the street, surrounded by a crowd of people. (When the camera shows his face, we see that it is not an actor but an actual poet, Andrei Voznesensky.)

The second part of the film is set in the 1970s. The same three women are now Muscovites, just as they wanted to be. But the excitement of the three provincial girls who came to make it in the capital has been superseded by the practicalities of day-to-day life: work, raising children, dealing with relationships. They have achieved what they wanted, although in some cases it was a short-lived victory, or did not bring them the happiness they desired. The most interesting things are happening to Katya, who having concluded that she was probably destined to spend her life without a "life partner", meets a man on a local train…

Moscow Does Not Believe in Tears evokes many memories in anyone who has lived in the USSR. There is the move from village to big city. The three girls who came to Moscow to pursue their dreams are *limitchiki* – or rather, the feminine equivalent, *limitchitsy*. These are Soviet era *Gastarbeiter*, only not from abroad: rather they would be people from small towns or villages who would come to the big cities, preferably Moscow, prepared to do hard and dirty work in the hope of a better life. There was no freedom of movement in the USSR, and once you had your registration (*propiska*) in one place, you couldn't simply move to a "better" area and get a job and a registration there. If you wanted to move to a big city, you would have to do the dirty jobs that the locals wouldn't do, as one of the "limited" (hence the name *limitchiki*) number of workers allowed to participate in this scheme. After a while, you could find a way to stay in the city permanently, either by working a certain number of years or by getting married to someone with a local registration.

Talking of *limitchiki*, I am reminded of my father's parents. Having left their village near Ryazan, which had been devastated by the twin catastrophes of the Second World War and years of Soviet agriculture, they brought their three children to Moscow, as did so many other peasants. They were housed, together with similar families, in a room in the so-called "barracks" that hosted migrant workers. While the parents were at work, the children ran free after school. There was a lot of solidarity between the families, and knocking on another family's door while one's own parents were at work would immediately get a child invited in for lunch. My grandmother and grandfather when I knew them were happy people: they were happy to have their own flat, to have enough to eat, to have black and red caviar on their table at celebrations (even though so many things were scarce, caviar was always available in Soviet times, although it was expensive), to have a colour TV and spend their spare time pickling cucumbers and making pies.

By the way, in flagrant violation of the Russian constitution, Moscow remains a closed city where registration is still not available to everyone. If you want to come and work in the Russian capital, almost all jobs require you to have Moscow registration already. Therefore those who want to move to Moscow have to play all sorts of tricks to get this piece of paper with a stamp.

The director of *Moscow Does Not Believe in Tears*, Vladimir Menshov, also knew first-hand what it was like for a provincial lad to try to make his way in the capital. It took him four attempts to enrol in the Moscow filmmakers' school, and he spent those four years working at a factory as a metal turner, plus a spell in a coal mine in Vorkuta in the Arctic Circle.

Menshov came to the capital that "did not trust tears" with a dream of conquering it: "When I first came to Moscow it was a shock, it was a dream city, an ungraspable city. When I arrived I was ready to get to my knees and kiss the ground, even if the ground was the platform of a train station."

He wanted to attract a big audience. He later said that when he was starting his career he liked to imagine his films shown to a packed Rossia, a huge cinema in central Moscow with a seating capacity of over 2,000.

Moscow Does Not Believe in Tears achieved just that – spontaneous success. Spontaneity was not exactly a very Soviet thing. Some works of art were intended to be, and promoted to be, successes, since they served an ideological purpose. But Menshov's film was not the Soviet critics' choice, nor the government ideologues' choice. It was the people's choice. What people wanted was bittersweet drama, a fairytale of a Soviet Cinderella with touches of comedy.

The Russian public loved the movie from the start. In 1980 it beat all other films at the USSR box office, with 90 million people seeing it in the cinema. The low-key, unpompous tone of the movie, the absence of politics, the focus on the lives of ordinary people drew in the audience across the whole Soviet Union. They could relate to so many issues and situations in the film: looking for a better life in a big city, dealing with alcoholic husbands, raising a child on one's own. Also the friendship that starts in a hostel and lasts through the years. A strong self-made woman, very lonely in a male-dominated society. And, of course, happy endings were not at all the norm in Soviet melodramas, so this film's positive note gave the viewers some much-needed hope.

In the meantime, neither Menshov's colleagues nor the critics were convinced. The critics found the film sentimental and implausible. The opinions of Soviet critics are usually not worth considering, but maybe they had a point on this occasion. Was the public too eager to swallow the bittersweet medicine with its blend of fairy tale and kitchen-sink drama? Even Alexei Batalov, the actor who played Gosha, the "practically" perfect man who appears in Katya's life, thought the movie was implausible, and the happy ending dubious. He later said, possibly tongue-in-cheek, that women had not looked closely at his character, whose appearance "eases the poor woman's suffering". "Gosha left his first wife, he accosts a strange woman on a train, he drinks, he fights…" "on day three he might have just hit her on the head with a bottle. Why not?" Batalov said.

As for the cinema world, we can only guess why the attitude was so hostile. Menshov's explanation was as follows: "It was not only envy, but I messed with the accepted customs of film-making. One was that cinema should be social and covertly oppositional. And another one was that a film which aimed to please the audience was a second-rate film. A good film was one you showed to your 20 friends, who afterwards gave you a firm handshake and looked you understandingly in the eye." What probably irritated Menshov's colleagues, among other things, was his dismissive view of Soviet counter-culture. In the first part of the film we are about to enter the 1960s, a time of what dissident historian Andrei Amalrik called "cultural opposition", when young writers, poets and artists started to challenge Soviet aesthetics. Several young poets attracted huge crowds with their public readings. But the girls in Menshov's film could not care less for the poets reading their poems on Mayakovsky Square. They listen for a bit, shrug their shoulders in confusion, and go off. What really excites them is to see movie stars entering a cinema. The same happens at a party at the professor's flat, where a conversation started by a young poet peters out because no one is interested, and it's the ice hockey star who gets all the attention.

Whatever happened to that young poet at the professor's table? By the second part, we have forgotten all about him. Life in the film goes on regardless of any political events or cultural movements between 1958 and 1978. Isn't this the way most people in the Soviet Union lived, shrugging their shoulders in confusion at anything beyond their day-to-day worries? The dissidents of the USSR, as well as the cultural and scientific elite, were just as far away from "the people" – *narod* – as were the political thinkers in pre-revolutionary Russia. The majority of people in the USSR did not participate in political protests or underground culture movements – were not even aware of them, in fact.

What makes Russians of different generations still love this film is partly post-Soviet nostalgia, this phenomenon of pining for the old USSR when "living conditions were more equal, people were nicer, grass was greener and all our enemies were scared of us". The view the film gives of the Soviet past is in soft focus, cosy and convenient, and therefore it feeds this nostalgia. For some viewers who grew up in the USSR, the city as shown in *Moscow Does Not Believe in Tears* has become what Moscow was for Chekhov's three sisters – something of a lost paradise.

But what is also important is that the film provides a bridge to the past – the Soviet past, the only past the Russians remember, since pre-Soviet Russia is such a lost world. A sense of the past and the connection between generations is easily lost in a Russia that during the twentieth century underwent so many calamities and major upheavals. I remember how impressed I was when I came to England to see people with their family trees on the wall. Families in Russia have been torn apart, separated and dislodged, so it was unusual to know the names of one's great-grandparents, let alone ancestors further back. You would lose your relatives who emigrated after the revolution, those killed in wars, those who perished in prisons, those who were moved by force – and, during the time of Stalin, if a relative was arrested the most sensible thing to do would be to lose all contact with that branch of the family.

In a post-Soviet period of sudden fragmentation there is a tendency, not only in Russia but also in other former Soviet bloc countries, to hold on to those cultural references from a time of little choice as something unifying, providing a sensation of a common past, of belonging to a family.

The film is full of little details of day-to-day Moscow life. Take the party at the professor's apartment that Ludmilla organizes, when she and Katya pretend to be the professor's daughters. We are in the late 1950s, and change is in the air. At the table there is a young, upcoming, complacent TV cameraman, who says that television will soon replace all other artforms. A young poet disagrees. A 40-something party official, Anton, has brought some Kamchatka crabs and other expensive delicacies. He is trying to flirt with the girls, but spends most of his time in the loo.

We see the generation gap when Anton says, referring to the change from Stalin's bloodthirsty dictatorship to Khrushchev's less harsh leadership: "Now you cannot move for rebels, who like nothing more than to criticize the older generation. They keep asking us: why did you tolerate everything in silence? Now it is easy to talk. I would like to see what they would have done in our times." "*We* would not have been silent," answers the young poet.

There are plenty of other little episodes that are vignettes of life in the Soviet Union, such as when Katya, working at the factory in the first part of the film, learns how to solve simple problems with her equipment herself, just so as not to have to wait forever for a technician. Again, the episode when a TV crew comes to the plant where

Katya is working, with a view to making a typical Soviet report from a factory where happy workers find fulfilment in their jobs and look forward to returning to the factory after finishing university. Katya is chosen to be interviewed, and is given a piece of paper with notes on what she should say, but she goes completely off-script, saying that she is only doing her new job because she has been told to by her supervisor, not because it is more creative, and that she has no plans to return to the factory unless she fails her university exams.

When Katya's lover, the TV cameraman who initially thought she was a professor's daughter, discovers she is working at a factory and calls her a "heroine of labour", he does not mean it as a compliment. Despite the official state adulation of workers and collective farmers, working at a factory would certainly be sneered at by what might loosely be called the Soviet Union's middle class. When Katya discovers she is pregnant and asks her lover to find a doctor, he sends her to the factory: "Shouldn't they look after workers' health?"

Even the small characters in the film are important. Menshov once said: "I feel a fraud if I hire an actor and he has no acting to do." The mother of the cameraman who seduces Katya grovels to her when she thinks that Katya is a professor's daughter, but gives her the cold shoulder when she finds out she is not. The *babushka* guard at the hostel is very severe with everyone, but for some reason is besotted with Ludmilla – and as she runs to fetch her to the phone, a young couple take their chance to sneak inside…

There is an episode when Ludmilla and Katya see actors entering a cinema through the throng of admirers and join in. All the celebrities are actually famous actors playing themselves. The two girls strike up a conversation with someone who says he is also starting out as an actor. He tells them his name, but remarks that it wouldn't mean anything to them. The two girls shake their heads. We are still in the late 1950s, of course. But to the Russian audience of the 1980s the name of Innokenty Smoktunovsky, Hamlet in the famous Kozintsev film, would be as instantly recognizable as Laurence Olivier's in Britain.

The main characters are beautifully acted. I really sympathize with Katya's character, her independence, her determination, her naivety – and her mixture of impulsiveness and self-control. Vera Alentova brilliantly depicts Katya's pain and confusion in the first part of the movie, and her loneliness in the second part, 20 years later, just as she reaches the summit of her profession.

Gosha (Alexei Batalov), the man who appears in Katya's life when she is already a factory director and the mother of a grown-up girl, is happy to take over in the kitchen when he sees Katya is tired – but he is not prepared to take instructions from her and fails to cope with the fact that she earns more than he does.

There is a moment in the movie that puzzled my English husband. After a misunderstanding, Gosha disappears. Katya is inconsolable. Her old hostel friends come to help. The husband of Tonya, the sweet country girl, vows to track Gosha down, and when he does, Gosha is not in good shape. He has clearly not left his flat for a week, drinking to drown his disappointment. He opens the door to Nikolai and, without saying a word, goes back to the table and pours a second glass of vodka. Nikolai approaches, drinks the vodka in one go, and smells the dry fish that is lying on the table, without actually eating it. This wins the man's trust, so he stretches out his hand, introducing himself: "Gosha".

Seeing the dry fish episode, my husband asked: "What is he doing?" I had to explain that Nikolai is a hard man who can hold his drink, but who understands the notion that drinking without eating is only for alcoholics. By smelling the fish, he acknowledges this, but shows that the moment is not for eating but for serious conversation. It was funny for me to see from some other viewers' reviews that it was also one of their favourite episodes in the movie. Not so much because of the dry fish, but because according to them it shows Russians' ability to immediately relate to strangers.

The idea that it is never too late to start again is not very present in Russian movies, or Russian culture. Maybe what made *Moscow Does Not Believe in Tears* so loved is above all the underlying motif of hope. "Believe me, when you are 40, you will think your life is only beginning," says party official Anton at Ludmilla and Katya's party in the first part of the movie. Everyone else at the table is still very young, and they do not pay much attention to his words.

Moscow Does Not Believe in Tears won the Oscar for Best Foreign Language Film in 1981. As the director was not allowed out of the country, a suited KGB-type from the Soviet embassy came on stage to receive the award, accompanied by hilarity from the audience and, the next day, sarcastic remarks in the Western press.

Meanwhile, knowing his film had been nominated, Menshov was

trying to tune in to the Voice of America on the day of the Oscars ceremony to find out what was going on, but the signal was constantly being jammed, so he was left in the dark. The next day, which was April 1, he received a phone call telling him he had won, and he thought someone was having him on.

Some critics called the film's success a triumph for Soviet propaganda. This I think is a bit harsh. Maybe it would be better to call it a human face peeking out from behind the Iron Curtain?

Language notes:

"Хэллоу! Общежитие слушает!" – Ludmilla is pretending she is a Muscovite herself, and not a *limitchitsa*, so as not to scare off a potential suitor. The hostel has only one phone, the one on the desk of the scary *babushka* overseer. When she picks up, the *babushka's* standard opening is "The hostel is listening!" When Ludmilla gives out her number, she doesn't want people to know she lives in a hostel, so she remonstrates, saying: "Can't you say [in English] 'Hello?'" The guard, who is strict with the other students, but somehow charmed by Ludmilla, tries hard to comply, managing a "Hello?" in English when picking up – but then ruining it by adding in Russian "The hostel is listening!"

"Не учи меня жить, лучше помоги материально!" – "Don't teach me how to live, better help me with money!" – Ludmilla is not about to listen to Tonya's boyfriend's advice on how to behave.

"А заодно запомни, что всё и всегда я буду решать сам. На том простом основании, что я – мужчина." "Just remember that I alone will always decide everything, simply because I am a man." – The words of Gosha, the man who finally comes to save Katya from loneliness.

"Ах, это, это я люблю. Но только в нерабочее время и под хорошую закуску." – "Ah, this I do like. But only when not working, and with proper food." – In their first conversation, as Gosha tries to convince Katya of his virtues, she asks him if he likes drinking, and this is his answer.

"Да у меня практически нет недостатков." – "I have practically no shortcomings," says Gosha, but he is actually being a bit ironic (I think).

"И ляпай! Но ляпай уверенно! Это у них назывется эксцентричностью!" – "Well, say stupid things! But say them with confidence! They call it being eccentric!" – Ludmilla explains to Katya the art of pretending one is a Muscovite, and not a girl from the provinces.

"Как там погода? – С утра шёл дождь." "What's the weather like? – It's been raining all day." – This is the first exchange between Gosha and Nikolai after that vodka-drinking fish-smelling episode that I have described earlier. Even for a Russian, it is strange and funny that these should be the first phrases that two people who have never met should say to each other. But it also means that the level of confidence has been established (by drinking vodka and smelling the fish), to the point that long explanations and introductions are not necessary.

"Ну, ладно, ладно. Москва слезам не верит." – "OK, OK. Moscow doesn't trust tears," says Ludmilla, trying to comfort Katya when the new man in her life disappears.

"Нет, работаем мы в разных местах, но жить, я надеюсь, будем вместе." – "No, we are working in different places, but I hope we will live together." – Gosha announces this at his first dinner at Katya's house, to Katya's daughter's shock.

YEMELYA THE SIMPLETON

ЕМЕЛЯ-ДУРАЧОК

When I reread Russian folk tales, I am always surprised at how much I enjoy them. But how would I not? Reliving that magic world that is part of every Russian's earliest childhood brings back memories of waking up in the morning to see a big dish of freshly baked aromatic cabbage pies... or putting three kopeks into a street soda machine, and feeling your throat get particularly dry while watching the syrup and fizzy water fill the glass... or meeting the train from the far north arriving at a Moscow station, the scent of the lilac blossom I am holding in my hands mixing with the smell of soot...

The clever fox and the stupid bear, the round bread Kolobok who goes off into the woods looking for adventures; Prince Ivan and his loyal Grey Wolf; the wicked old magician Kashchei the Deathless, who arrives like a tornado stealing beautiful ladies and is impossible to kill, unless you know where his death is hidden – in a needle, within an egg, inside a duck that is hiding in a big tree; the Frog Princess who creates magic lakes with swans with a wave of her sleeve; the evil witch Baba Yaga who lives in the deepest woods in a log cabin on hen's feet and likes to eat little children and wandering knights...

And of course Yemelya and his magic pike, and his Russian stove that can double as a means of transport.

This fairy tale belongs to the genre of stories about a "simpleton", a "fool", in Russian "durak", also called affectionately "durachyok". The universal plot of a naive, sometimes lazy, sometimes shrewd misfit in this folk tale acquires typically Russian features.

While his brothers are working, Yemelya spends the whole day lying on a stove. Here I should explain what a Russian stove – печь – is. The centrepiece of every Russian peasant's house, around which the life of the family revolves both physically and metaphorically, it serves both as heater and oven. It is a huge thing in the middle of the logwood house, made of bricks, fed with wood, designed to retain heat for as long as possible, which is achieved not only by the action of the bricks, but by channelling hot air through passages in its structure. It gives out a steady, constant heat, so that the fuel only needs to be added a couple of times a day, and the peasant's *izba* stays warm even through the bitterly cold winter days. The food inside the oven cooks to perfection. There is a nice warm sleeping place above the stove, usually occupied by the most privileged members of the family: the grandparents, who can warm their rheumatic joints there. Here it is occupied by the simpleton Yemelya, and it is very hard to convince him to get down and help around the house, although he does do so when he is promised sweets from the market, or a pair of red boots.

One winter day, while his brothers are away on business, Yemelya is sent by the women of the house to fetch water. Yemelya collects a couple of buckets and an axe (even an idiot knows you need an axe when you go to get water in Russia) and sets off to the frozen river. He makes a hole in the ice (with the axe). After filling the buckets, he stares for a while into the river's dark water. Suddenly he sees a pike. Somehow he manages to catch it. The pike is a magic fish, and it talks to Yemelya, begging him to let it go, and promising that if he does, his every wish will come true, all he has to do is say: "By the pike's command, by my wish!" To test this, he tells the buckets of water to go home by themselves – and off they go. So Yemelya lets the pike go, and heads back home with his new magic powers.

From then on he can order the axe to chop wood or the sledge to move without horses. When called to see the tsar who has heard about his magic powers and is keen to meet him, he does not even have to leave his favourite nook on top of the stove, as the stove leaves the house and drives where Yemelya tells it to – "by the pike's command, by my wish!"

At the tsar's palace Yemelya's attention is caught by the ruler's beautiful daughter... And so the fairy tale continues.

Why, of all the folk tales, have I chosen this one? Well, it was not an easy choice. There are a great many fairy tales which every Russian knows by heart. Some are more magical than Yemelya the Simpleton, and others are more colourful. There are also some that are more pagan and spooky, which are in fact not particularly well-known in Russia, possibly because they were not much publicized during Soviet times. They are the ones that seem to make it into the English-language collections though. My husband gave Arthur Ransome's collection *Old Peter's Russian Tales* to the teenage daughter of a friend – after reading which, the friend said, the daughter would "probably never sleep again". Was it that spooky fairy tale about the orphan girl Vasilisa the Beautiful that did it? Just before she died,

Vasilisa's mother gave her a doll, and told her that if ever she needed help, she should give the doll food and ask her for advice. The doll would open her eyes, eat the food, and tell Vasilisa not to worry and to go to bed, and the next morning all the impossibly hard tasks – that first her stepmother, and later the evil witch Baba Yaga had set her – had been completed...

Going back to the tale of Yemelya, I like it because it is light-hearted, entertaining, slightly subversive, very rustic, mystical if you choose to see it that way, and self-critical if you want to see it that way.

I like the slightly random and almost Zen feel of this tale. Some Russians even consider it to be anti-Russian, possibly invented in antiquity by some spy in a subversive attempt to present the Russians as lazy and looking for magic solutions (seriously, you can find these opinions on the internet). My (English) husband, having read it, thought it was a terribly immoral and reprehensible story of someone who is showered with wealth and all the good things in life for no good reason at all, a bit like the wholesale reallocation of USSR state property that lies behind the emergence of today's Russian "oligarchs".

Is this a tale about passivity, lack of drive, relying on luck and hoping that someone else is going to come and do everything for you? Western-oriented and self-critical Russians lament these features in their people and like to quote the twelfth-century *Tale of Bygone Years*, Russia's earliest surviving chronicle. This manuscript mentions how in the ninth century, after a lot of bloody conflicts between various minor rulers, ancient Russians turned to the Vikings with the following words: "Our land is big and plentiful but there is no order in it. Come to rule and possess us."

Many Russian western-minded philosophers and journalists see depressing traits in Russian fairy tales, particularly those about lucky fools: the inability and unwillingness to take responsibility, waiting for the impulse for action to come from somewhere else, the inveterate fatalism.

I could pursue the topic of Russians' lack of faith that their own individual or collective actions can bring about any change in their lives, and of a fatalism born of historic and personal experience and reflected in fairy tales in which a knight comes to a crossroads, where there is a stone that says: "Go right and lose your horse, go left and lose your head, go straight and lose yourself". The never-ending discussion about Russian fatalism is a self-fulfilling prophecy, and does no good to the many people in Russia who are actually trying to do something – the journalists who choose to do their jobs properly, despite the danger of being beaten up or killed (Russia maintains its place within the top 10 most dangerous countries for journalists); opposition leader and anti-corruption fighter Alexei Navalny, described by the *Wall Street Journal* as "the man Vladimir Putin fears most"; the "Blue Buckets" association of drivers highlighting the impunity of politicians and plutocrats who cause accidents by driving around with flashing sirens and invading the oncoming traffic lane. The masses of people who came out onto the streets to protest against the falsifications at the 2011–2012 elections, risking rough treatment from riot police, are hardly fatalists. As for lack of initiative, I think Russians showed plenty of resourcefulness when, in the early 1990s, everybody lost their jobs overnight – when engineers had to learn to sew bootleg jeans and nuclear scientists had to find jobs as drivers.

If inertia is rewarded in the tale of Yemelya, so in other stories are generosity, curiosity, resourcefulness, kindness, self-sacrifice and living in harmony with the natural world. The good-natured girl who treats everyone politely, including an apple tree and a talking oven, ends up loaded with wealth and affection, while the haughty girl comes to regret her rudeness. Prince Ivan spares the hare, the duck and the fish when they plead for their lives, and they come to his rescue when he most needs them. Wise Yelena is frustrated at having a commonplace and not very bright husband, Ivan, until she is made to realize he possesses an important quality that she is missing – a good heart.

And as for that knight at the crossroads where each of the three roads offers a less than enticing prospect, it is worth remembering that the knight usually does not choose the easy path where he could lose his horse, although that seems like an obvious choice. Not because he is stupid, but because the knight understands that losing the horse would eventually make him perish too. The knight chooses the road that promises death not out of fatalism, but to challenge the prophecy – and, needless to say, at the end of the fairy tale always comes back alive.

But let us come back to Yemelya, and look at him from a slightly different perspective. As someone interested in Eastern philosophies, I cannot help noticing the Daoist aspect of the Simpleton in Russian tales. The central concept of Daoism is "wu wei", "without action". The idea is that instead of imposing one's own will on the world, involving (fruitless) effort, one should act just as a planet turns, or a tree grows – effortlessly and naturally. It also involves knowing when to act, and when not to act, and it is not only mystical but practical, because when you achieve this vision, you turn up at the right place at the right time, know what action to take, and are immune to any dangers.

So, while his brothers are off somewhere working, trying uselessly to impose their will on the Dao, Yemelya is practising the sweet "wu wei" on top of a stove. Going with the flow of the law of nature, he finds himself at the right place at the right time: peering into a hole in the icy river (who else would be doing this, if not a simpleton?) just as a magic pike peeps out of the water. An "intelligent" person knows what he is going to see in a dark hole in the ice, and will not be wasting time staring into it. It is the "fool" who approaches the unknown without any preconceptions.

The story of three brothers, one of whom is thought by all to be an idiot, but has both a heart of gold and the kind of inner wisdom that the other two do not possess, is a running theme in Russian fairy tales. It does not happen in the story of Yemelya, but usually in such tales the intelligent and sensible brothers at some point try to kill the "fool" and take away any treasure he got through his "foolishness", which they failed to get through their exertions. Generally the fool comes back to life, after being sprinkled with the magic "water of life" (nothing to do with vodka), to reassert his rights.

And then, of course, stories about how life does not depend on an individual's will or work make for more entertaining listening. It is not that those who tell the story and those who listen to it do not understand that such things do not happen in real life, or that Yemelya has not earned what he gets. But it *is* a magic tale. It has its tongue in its cheek. It would be boring to have a tale about someone who has worked hard, lived a proper life, got married, had children, accumulated wealth... What is entertaining about that? Russian tales tend to have flawed heroes, which makes them more fun to read about.

The story of Yemelya is a magic tale, but the magic aspect is very childlike. It has none of the magical characters of many Russian folk tales, such as three-headed dragons or firebirds. All the miracles in the tale of Yemelya have to do with ordinary things: water buckets that can walk home, a sledge that moves without a horse, an axe that chops wood all by itself. Not scary, not very believable, but childlike and entertaining.

The winter, the hole in the ice of the river and the stove give this tale its particular Russian feel. The pike that Yemelya caught is not generally considered a delicacy, but Russians like to use it for soup – *ukhá*. And of course, winter in Russia is a time when there is no work in the fields, and the long dark evenings provide the perfect setting for telling tales.

You cannot talk about the genre of tales about "simpletons" without mentioning the role that the *yurodivy*, the "holy fool" – has played in Russian culture. Holy fools were those who rejected (or fell out of) normal life to live on the street, abasing themselves completely, going around in rags and acquiring a reputation for being clairvoyants and close to God. This figure, present in many traditions and religions, has been very important in Russia. Being mad or simulating madness helped the *yurodivy* to detach himself from society and the social hierarchy. They were believed to be divinely inspired, and their utterances, usually in the form of riddles, were given a lot of attention. Harming a holy fool was considered a terrible sin, and even the tsars listened to what they had to say.

The multicoloured cupolas in Red Square in Moscow, such a trademark image of Moscow and Russia, belong to St Basil's Cathedral, built by order of Ivan the Terrible specifically to accommodate the body of a holy fool, Basil – or rather Vasily – who used to wander around Red Square naked, giving the tsar a hard time each time he saw him go past for not paying sufficient attention to the church and generally for not being a very good Christian.

One of the landmarks of Soviet cinema is the 1938 film *By the Pike's Command*, by Alexander Rou, which started a whole tradition of Russian magic films, full of special effects (state of the art at the time). The ideological victory of Yemelya (who in this film is not at all lazy, but rather unfortunate and exploited by the tsarist regime) over the tsar manifests itself in his winning the heart of the tsar's daughter, the spoiled, bad-tempered Nesmeyana ("Neverlaughs").

You can find a reference to this tale in a Russian make of car-seat heaters called Yemelya (it is twenty degrees below zero outside, but you are nice and comfortable in your car, as though it was a magic Russian stove that you were driving around).

Also, the unprecedented feat of reaching the North Pole in motorized vehicles, having travelled 1,100 kilometres across drift ice, was achieved by special trucks called Yemelya, after the character who did not like to leave his stove and preferred to travel with it.

Language notes:

"По щучьему велению…" – "By the pike's command" – you can use this phrase when talking about something good that comes out of nowhere, as if by magic – "как будто по щучьему велению". Or to tell someone he is lazy and wants everything to happen by magic, "by the pike's command".

Щука – pike. A desirable catch for Russian fishermen, as its gamey flesh is considered a delicacy. As they can be as much as 1.8 metres long, catching a big pike is something to boast about. Gefilte fish is a staple dish among Russian Jews, and is often made with pike.

Печь (печка) – a stove or a wooden oven.

"Мели Емеля – твоя неделя" – "Keep talking, Yemelya – you're on a roll." This expression is not in the story of Yemelya and the Magic Pike, but is one most people think of as being connected with the tale. "Молоть" – to mill – can also mean to talk rubbish, "молоть языком", to mill with the tongue. This expression means you do not believe a single word of what someone is saying.

"Отпусти меня, я тебе пригожусь!" – "Let me go, I will be of service to you!" – this is what the pike says to Yemelya, and this is what many magic animals say to those who catch them in other Russian tales. Wise characters let the animals go, and then in times of trouble the animals come to their aid.

"Мне неохота" – "I don't feel like it" – typical of Yemelya, who would rather stay lazing on the stove.

"Ни в сказке сказать, ни пером описать" – "Impossible to tell in a tale or to describe with a quill" – used in many fairy tales, about something or someone extraordinary beautiful.

"Пир на весь мир" – "A feast for the whole world" – the young lovers are happily together, and the whole world is happy

"Вот и сказке конец, а кто слушал, молодец" – "this is the end of a fairy tale, good for the one who was listening" – a common ending for a fairy tale (although I personally prefer "и я там был, мёд-пиво пил, по усам текло, а в рот не попало" – "I was there too, I drank honey and beer, it poured down my moustache, but never reached my mouth").

Mikhail Zhvanetsky

Михаил Жванецкий

What sort of images do big crayfish conjure up for you? Very big crayfish which were five roubles in the market yesterday? What about the much smaller crayfish that are three roubles today? Have I lost you already?

Russians of my generation and older know exactly which crayfish I am talking about: the crayfish in Mikhail Zhvanetsky's famous comic monologue. "Yesterday's cost five roubles... they were big... but that was yesterday... very big, though... but it was yesterday, and today's are three roubles – they're small, but three roubles. But there they are..."

In the USSR of the 1980s you saw theatres full of people in tears of laughter at this monologue. Why? I did not understand this when I was younger, and didn't find it particularly funny. Now looking back on it I can see better how people could relate to someone lost in pointless reflections, wasting his brain on choosing between options none of which were in fact available. Particularly when the stage version, slightly different from the written version of this monologue, went on: "If only I had five roubles yesterday... Not that I have three roubles today..."

Mikhail Zhvanetsky, like many other comics and satirists and writers (including Ilf and Petrov, the authors of *The Twelve Chairs*), comes from the city of Odessa. An engineer by profession, Zhvanetsky started writing short comic stories while working in the port of Odessa in the early 1960s. When the legendary comic actor Arkady Raikin was on tour in Odessa, he read Zhvanetsky's stories and liked them so much that he invited him to come to Leningrad and work as a scriptwriter for his theatre.

This theatre, called The Leningrad Theatre of Vignettes, was held together by the genius of Raikin, and its repertoire consisted entirely of comic and satirical dialogues and short plays.

Moving first to Leningrad and later to Moscow, Zhvanetsky spent a decade writing comic sketches for other performers before deciding to go on stage and read his own work; and this is what he has been doing since, for around 40 years now. Dressed immaculately, and recently rather overexuberantly, the satirist (who once said of himself: "I can say in all certainty: I will never be tall. Nor handsome") never recites his stories from memory. He adjusts his glasses, gets a few slightly crumpled-looking handwritten pieces of paper out of the well-worn yellow and brown briefcase he inherited from his father – a doctor – and reads them out. And the public starts laughing even before he says anything really funny, simply because they love Zhvanetsky and he has been part of their past, as well as their chaotic present.

Someone who asks, "Normal'no, Grigory?" expects the reply "Otlichno, Konstantin!" ["Everything OK, Grigory?" – "Great, Konstantin!"], not because the two people conversing are actually called Grigory and Konstantin, but because they are quoting Zhvanetsky's 1970s sketch about two men who, every time they are overcome by Soviet reality where nothing works as it should, just have a shot of vodka, after which everything seems bearable, and even quite excellent.

Or someone may say "vkus – spetsifichesky" – "it tastes… peculiar", without even remembering exactly where the phrase came from (it came from Zhvanetsky's story about *defitsit* – rare foods that were difficult to get during the Soviet times, whose taste had almost been forgotten, and is hard to describe).

Zhvanetsky is a writer more than a performer, and one who pays great attention to style. But he is also a Jewish son of Odessa, the port on the Black Sea famous for its European architecture, its mix of cultures (Russian, Jewish, Ukrainian and Greek, at least) and its people's distinctive vocabulary and way of speaking and their pride in their sense of humour. Zhvanetsky's language is primarily "classical" Russian, influenced by his roots in the sense that "the Jewish style is to formulate briefly, colourfully and concisely. This is called 'Frame it and memorize it for life.'" But when Zhvanetsky talks about Odessa, he tells his city's stories in its dialect and with its accent.

The Odessa dialect is distinctive for its frivolous attitude to grammar, such as noun declensions and the use of prepositions. Interjecting phrases with "taki da". Some very imaginative expressions, for example "*dve bol'shie raznitsy*" – "two big differences", meaning "a big difference", that is now used all over Russia. It mixes Yiddish and Ukrainian words with criminal jargon, Odessa having always been famous for its gangs.

And then there is the Odessa accent, with the Ukrainian "h" where Russians would have "g", "sh" instead of "s", long Jewish vowels and sing-song; the soft non-rolling "r" typical of Jewish Russians' speech; an intonation that rises almost indignantly towards the end of the phrase, and then falls suddenly.

Odessans are also famous for answering a question with another question, for verbally and physically invading your personal space, for loving to talk, for pausing between phrases while telling a story so that the listener can picture the scene.

Although his Odessa accent is mild, it becomes more pronounced when Zhvanetsky reads his stories about the city, for example "How They Play Practical Jokes in Odessa":

"[a brass band arrives on the doorstep of un unsuspecting tenant]

Bandmaster (takes off his hat politely): Ai-iai-iai, I have heard! Such a tragedy!
Tenant: What tragedy?
Bandmaster: You have a funeral?
Tenant: Funeral?
Bandmaster: Number 6 Richelieu Street, flat seven?
Tenant: Yes.
Bandmaster: Well?
Tenant: What?
Bandmaster: Is there going to be a funeral?
Tenant: Whose?
…
Trombone: Misha, is anything going to happen here, or shall we destroy this shack and break it in two? I am an invalid, as you know.
Brigadier: Zhora, do not get exasperated. These people have suffered a great tragedy, they want to haggle. Name your price, we will talk like cultured people. You have not heard our sound yet.
Tenant: I can imagine it…

[after a long argument, the tenant finally realizes he will not be able to get rid of the band and gives in]

Tenant: How much for a funeral?
Bandmaster: With honours?
Tenant: Yes.
Bandmaster: Without any rush?
Tenant: Yes.
Bandmaster: Five roubles each.

Tenant: And what if there is no dead body?
Bandmaster: Three roubles each, although that would be humiliating.
Tenant: OK, it's a deal. Play and sing: in memory of Sigizmund Lazarevich and his sister from Kishinev.

[as the orchestra is playing, a body is being carried in the vicinity – that of a neighbour Sigizmund Lazarevich, passed out drunk, who has just been celebrating his birthday]."

Zhvanetsky says that he needs around three to four hours to write a piece, but then to get the right tone when reading it from the stage takes him at least a year.

He is famous for his aphorisms ("One awkward move, and you are a father", "In small doses, alcohol is harmless in any quantity").

He is loved for his charm and an energy that has not diminished with age; for the melancholy that seeps through his humour; for being around for so long; for always being censored and perceived as someone who has not "sold out" and doesn't shift with the winds of change. He is reflective in that double Russian-Jewish way and is, touchingly, just a little bit provincial.

Zhvanetsky has been lamenting the loss of his audience, saying that his prime listeners were the Soviet middle class, those engineers (a huge proportion of the Soviet population were engineers by training, even if their job consisted of shifting papers, rather than designing spaceships) who according to him left en masse in the 1980s and 1990s. His home city, of course, has seen a mass exodus to both the US and Israel. Has he ever thought of emigrating? He has. But what held him, he says, were not so much strong ropes that tied him to his country, but countless threads: "Too many things tie me to this place: the great literature; here I have experienced success, I have felt a connection. The ropes that tie me to this country I don't give a damn about. But I have had powerful threads."

But does Zhvanetsky really have a reason to complain about the loss of an audience? Now in his seventies, he gets a warm reception from younger fans. He says: "Some time ago people used to tell me: I love you, I admire you. Later, bit by bit, it turned into: my mum and dad love you, and now some people have already started saying: my granny adores you."

Not only does he still fill concert halls, once a month he appears on the television programme *Looking Out For the Country (Дежурный по стране)* where he comments on recent events, mainly using them as an excuse to digress about everything on earth. He answers questions from viewers and the studio audience. Projected onto big outdoor screens in a few locations in Moscow, he is somehow the same old Zhvanetsky, with the same old briefcase, as when he used to come on stage in provincial theatres. His comments on life in Russia in the early twenty-first century make Russians cry with laughter. "We are working non-stop, cyclically. We destroy what we have built. Then rebuild what we have destroyed. Then there is an equilibrium: we are building and destroying at the same speed. Then we build more than destroy. Then destroy more than build. And when we are about to leave the building site, we see that something not quite built has merged with something not quite destroyed, creating a strange mix of not-quite-built Socialism with underdeveloped Capitalism."

Some of Zhvanetsky's reflections are not at all funny, but rather sad and poignant. He says, for example, that nostalgia for Stalin is for a time when Soviet people really felt they could participate in the life of the country: "A Soviet person would inform on his neighbour, and that very evening the neighbour would be taken away. This was amazing efficiency. And this actually fulfils people's desires. Often the reason for informing would be to get somebody's flat, often to get somebody's job – it didn't matter! One report – and your enemy is in prison. Where else have you seen this, that a simple person can play such a role in his country! And what about informing on a scientist? Or on a deputy minister? Two or three people send their reports, and the person is in prison. I think this is where such admiration for Stalin stems from in the memory of those people who wrote those reports. The sense of their being in charge of the country."

As ever, his programmes are censored before they are released, but what is left out of *Looking Out For the Country* now finds its way onto the internet.

Zhvanetsky once compared a writer to a tomato, saying that he or she should mature in a hot, wide steppe and not in a greenhouse. Without doubt he is such a tomato, a healthy-looking, not terribly thin fellow who likes food, wine and women. He is not one of those stand-ups who wallow in their own histrionic anxiety. Zhvanetsky almost never talks about himself; he talks about the peculiarities of people, places, Russia, life.

Talking about what is missing in today's Russia, he says: "What I miss is that people come to an agreement, and build a theatre. Citizens come to an agreement and do something, construct something. Instead we come to an agreement, and then go to the authorities to ask for permission."

But he is not interested in a political career, although in the 1990s he had the chance of being part of the democratic political movement. He declined, he said, because he couldn't handle the insults in the parliamentary debates which so often became personal. This allows him to continue talking about the state as "them", as opposed to "us", the people:

"How do we make our state love its people? The people need to go away for a while. Leave the state without people, without us. And then something will happen, they will feel some sort of longing. Surely they will notice our absence? If only because they will not be able to feed themselves. The army will stay, the officials, the customs officers, the police – but we will not be around. We are gone. Our country is big, we can just hide in the woods."

But weighing up the present and the past, Zhvanetsky prefers life in today's Russia: "I hated it so much, felt so bad, during Soviet times that in spite of everything I do like it now. All my life I have lived among worn shoes, mended heels, socks with holes. Now if you look down, people are wearing good shoes. Life is getting better."

Language notes:

"Как сказал Жванецкий…" – "As Zhvanetsky said…"

On Russian politicians:

"Я не перестаю удивляться нашим политикам. Когда я впервые увидел шаг Майкла Джексона, когда человек шёл вперёд, а двигался назад, то думал, что это мастерство конкретного актёра. И восхищался. А у нас все так в политике могут!"

"Our politicians never fail to amaze me. When I saw Michael Jackson's walk for the first time, when he was walking forward but moving backwards, I thought it was his unique skill. And I admired it. But our politicians can all do that!"

On democracy in Russia:

"Наша демократия — это светофор, где горят три огня сразу. Как он горит, так мы и едем."
"Our democracy is like a traffic light with all three lights lit at the same time. The way it is lit is the way we drive".

"Наша свобода – это то, что мы делаем, когда никто не видит. Стены лифтов, туалеты вокзалов, колёса чужих машин..."
"Our freedom is what we do when nobody can see us. The walls of the lifts, train station toilets, the wheels of other people's cars..."

On life in Russia:

"Богатство в России напоминает стояние в пробках на очень дорогом авто."
"Being rich in Russia is like being stuck in a traffic jam in a very expensive car."

"Закон нашей жизни: не привыкнешь — подохнешь! не подохнешь — привыкнешь!"
"The law of our life: if you don't get used to it, you'll die, if you don't die, you'll get used to it!"

On Russian history:

"История России — борьба невежества с несправедливостью."
"The history of Russia is the fight of ignorance against injustice."

"Что касается управляющих, то на русской земле их было два типа: самодуры и самородки."
This is rather difficult to translate. Zhvanetsky uses two words that both have the root "сам" – "self". "Samodur" is someone who only listens to himself, and acts according to his own will, used for some-

one in power – a tyrant. "Samorodok" is a nugget of a precious metal, a word which is also used metaphorically about someone with a natural talent, a prodigy, usually with the additional meaning that this person is born into circumstances that impede his talent from developing and so he has to overcome them. "There have only been two types of manager on Russian soil: tyrants and prodigies."

"Это Россия – страна неограниченных возможностей и невозможных ограничений."
"That's Russia – the country of limitless possibilities and impossible limitations."

Mikhail Zadornov

Михаил Задорнов

When I was working as a teacher of Russian, I comforted my students by telling them that complete proficiency in Russian is impossible even for native Russian speakers. Russian grammar is so complicated that only a handful of academics speak and write perfect Russian. Everybody else does their best: Mikhail Gorbachev, for example, came from a peasant background, and his speech was full of mistakes that made educated Russians cringe. Then I would tell my students about a famous 1990s comedy sketch in which the USSR's first and only president gives his audience a Russian language lesson. The author of the skit was Mikhail Zadornov, a satirical writer and performer, who on that occasion showed that he was a good mimic too, imitating Gorbachev's soft South Russian accent and peppering his monologue with the president's idiosyncrasies of speech, adding a few more invented errors for good measure.

Zadornov is slim, tall, elegantly dressed, and he was brought up in Riga, Latvia. He is a former aviation engineer and the son of a writer. As I mention in another chapter, a great proportion of the Soviet "middle class" were engineers, even though their work was mainly administrative. But Zadornov actually worked as an aeronautical engineer. At the Moscow Aviation Institute he was popular with his fellow-students for his story-telling, and this is when he first dreamed of one day being able to earn his living telling funny stories to a bigger audience. The dream came true in the mid-1980s, after he started appearing on TV, and his popularity soared on the wave of *perestroika*.

We would stop whatever we were doing around the house when his quizzical face came on TV. His ironic take, what he was saying and how he was saying it, the way he drew our attention to familiar things and scrutinized them was hilarious and fascinating. Zadornov affected a state of constant amazement at the ridiculousness of the world around him. To Russians, his humour is perhaps a personification of what they imagine "English humour" to be: the ability to say funny things with a straight face, with a wry smile rather than laughing out loud, that famous English "phlegm" (as in being "phlegmatic", a quality which Russians like to attribute to the English).

His humour is of the raised-eyebrows variety. One of his famous monologues, written at the very beginning of *perestroika*, was called just that: "I don't understand" ("Я не понимаю"). It was written when the economy was still socialist and based on the government "plan", but the first cooperatives had started to appear: "The older I get, the less I understand. I don't understand how women complain both that there is no food in the shops and that it's impossible for them to lose weight. I do not understand many of our names for things, for example chocolates that are called Radium? Or a cake called Othello? And what kind of smell must eau de cologne "Sports-club" have?

"I do not understand anything in our socialist economy! For example, I do not understand what's so good about 'socialist competition'. How can a conveyor belt that produces socks for the right foot compete with a conveyor that produces socks for the left foot?

"I do not understand how over-fulfilling the Five-Year Plan can strengthen our economy. What do we do with all the door handles, if we produce three times more handles than doors? Of course, we could always use them for pans. Maybe this is why the washing machines you buy sometimes have aeroplane engines fitted, and when you switch them on you get the feeling they are about to take off; the vacuum-cleaners might have covers made out of missile shell-cases, and briefcases might have warehouse padlocks..."

If the world in general is absurd, Zadornov believes the Russian world is particularly absurd: "We are amazing people! We want to live like everybody else, but we don't want to be like anyone else. We honour the war dead, but do not pay those who survived. We always think ourselves cleverer than anyone else, and this is why we are always made fools of. Lazy and energetic, it is easier for us to invent an all-terrain vehicle than to repair roads. We honour Jesus and forget what he taught. We light a candle in church and pray for a higher interest rate."

His style is a bit journalistic. He collects absurdities (with help from the public) and presents them to the audience. Observations he makes on his travels, overheard conversations, newspaper classifieds, posters, names of shops: all are grist to his mill; such as a poster in the airport in Yakutsk, one of the coldest places on earth, from where tourists sometimes want to take home reindeer antlers as a souvenir: "Passengers with their antlers uncovered will not be allowed on the plane".

Or an ad for plastic windows: "You can kill a beaver and save a tree, but if you use our plastic windows you can save the beaver and the tree."

Or a bus route in Yuzhno-Sakhalinsk: "Mental Hospital – Cemetery" (this sums up the journey of life in Russia, says Zadornov).

Or a real estate ad: "Buy our 300m flat and get a free baseball cap".

Zadornov likes to call Russia "a great country with an unpredictable past". This is about both the revisionist trend in Russian history and the opening of the archives during *perestroika*, when previously suppressed facts of Russian history came to light.

Despite continuing to make fun of the absurdities of life in Russia, he has become in the last few years very critical of the West and its influence on the country after the break-up of the USSR, as well as of the behaviour of the former Soviet republics.

His anti-Western and particularly anti-US take on things fell on fruitful ground in the Russia of the first decade of the twenty-first century, when these sentiments became prevalent, a big change from the excitement of the 1990s, during the first opening of the borders and *perestroika*. In the early 1990s, when foreigners began to appear on the streets of Moscow, looking and behaving so differently to the locals that they might as well have come from Mars, there was not much suspicion or hostility, but mostly curiosity.

Later on things changed. The capitalist reforms and privatizations that led to most of the country's wealth accumulating in the hands of a few murky individuals left a lot of Russians unhappy. Those reforms were conducted in close collaboration with American think-tanks and successfully oversaw Russia's transition to a particular kind of capitalism. The sudden Western-backed reforms, the changed lifestyles, the loss of stability and the disintegration of the economy and social structures left many people nostalgic for the Soviet past. Then there was the 1998 financial crisis in Russia. While Western companies remember it for the money they lost when Russia defaulted on its debts, the Russians remember the Western companies escaping like rats from a sinking ship. Then Vladimir Putin came to power, and his government has been for the last 11 years igniting and encouraging xenophobia, nationalistic patriotism and anti-Western paranoia, in order to distract Russians from domestic problems – with mixed success.

Zadornov has captured this mood, encouraging his audience to be proud of all things Russian and calling for the restoration of worthwhile values from the Soviet times. His most famous saying in this respect is: "Запад стал для нас западнёй" – "The West for us became a trap" – playing on the similarity of the Russian words for *zapad* – the West, and *zapadnya* – a trap.

"Let's take a good look around us. What has come to our country from the West since the USSR collapsed? Soviet education was the best in the world. There was no obscene language in the theatre, in literature or on television. There was no food unfit for human consumption, but good for profits. There was no AIDS, no swine or bird flu. There was no pornography, sex-shops or blow-up women."

Is this the same man who used to tell his story about an American spy who is broken by Soviet reality and ends up in a mental asylum? It is sad to see Zadornov buying into this selective amnesia, a disease so widespread among Russians nowadays. Has he really forgotten what life was like in the USSR? Were there not more things lacking than sex-shops and blow-up women? (See for example the Soviet joke about a customer asking in a shop: "Don't you have any meat?" with the shop assistant answering: "This is the fish department – what we don't have is any fish."). Where did he get his food from in those days, anyway? Not from regular shops, probably, if it was fit for human consumption. There were some good things though – for example, Soviet chickens were real free-rangers. They were so muscular and hard, you'd think they had spent their lives running around the steppes. In the 1990s, when chicken legs started to be imported from the USA, they were promptly nicknamed "Bush's legs" and gave rise to jokes that they belonged to some multi-legged mutant chicken variety; and they tasted suspiciously soft and bland.

How many of Zadornov's views are genuine and how much they are influenced by a desire to please his public, or the government, can only be guessed at. But it seems incredible that someone in his position would not see either what a disaster the Soviet regime was for his country, or how counterproductive USSR-nostalgia is now.

Zadornov famously crossed out the US visa in his passport, having been irritated by the gratingly patriotic overtones of the 2002 Winter Olympics in Salt Lake City. Many people got the feeling that the event, held in the wake of September 11, was used as propaganda for the "war on terror". President Bush broke with protocol when he made his opening speech standing among the American athletes and not in the official box, and adding "on behalf of a proud, determined and grateful nation" to the usual opening lines. Many countries complained about their team members being constantly harassed by security. Zadornov said he did not regret the fact that he had ruined his chances of ever being granted another US visa, since there were a lot of places outside the US that he had yet to visit, such as the provincial Russian towns of Voronezh or Tambov. This gesture brought him a lot of kudos – a US visa is difficult to get for Russians, and for someone to dispose of it in such a cavalier fashion was regarded with awe.

Despite Zadornov's anti-Western views largely coinciding with those of the present Russian government, he is not known for being a particular friend of Putin's cabinet. He was not one of the actors, musicians, sports people and film directors who appeared in the 2012 United Russia campaign encouraging the population to vote for Putin; in fact in his blog he makes the ruling party the object of his most biting humour. But he was a good friend of Russia's late president Boris Yeltsin, playing tennis with him, going to the sauna and participating in some of Yeltsin's odder whims, like a swimming race in dressing gowns. This friendship in the 1990s apparently landed him an apartment in a prestigious Moscow building, mostly occupied by members of the government and their inner circle.

I suspect it was thanks to Zadornov's connections, as well as his popularity, that on the night of 31 December 1991, after the demise of the Soviet Union, when Gorbachev ceased to be president and Yeltsin had not yet been elected, Zadornov ended up addressing the people of Russia, the task usually assigned to a head of state. In his address he said: "Russia is a special country. Our national symbol has two eagle's heads, but three crowns. The main head, the one under the middle crown, has been blown away. We need to restore it. There is a good reason why one head is looking to the West and the other to the East, hinting that if we combine eastern wisdom with western rationalism we can have an amazing state that will not have left behind its high spiritual values, but will also have learnt to build its economy, with roads, swimming pools, hotels – to work no worse than they do in the West."

Mikhail Zadornov now has his own blog, in which he comments on political events in Russia. Many of his suggestions are common sense, and some are completely obnoxious, for example that "human-rights defenders in Russia have always been traitors." His readers' comments vary: "Mikhail, why don't YOU put yourself forward to be president, we would vote for you"; "Bastards like you with your humour brought about the collapse of the great Soviet state"; "You are so good when you tell your funny stories, why don't you just stick to that."

Now in his 60s, Zadornov is a big fan of yoga and looks a bit like a guru himself, particularly when he lets his beard grow. He follows an ayurvedic diet and is in good shape, sometimes showing off by doing the splits on stage.

One thing he does not want to be is a politician. "Today little depends on politicians, they are controlled by other forces. What we need are writers, film directors, actors, poets, artists – they can change the world, because they will change people's mentality, and politics will change with mentality. Politics itself cannot do anything nowadays. One thing it can do is not interfere."

In recent years Zadornov has been increasingly accused by his detractors of losing his originality, even of Internet-aided plagiarism. He is also seen by some as too "commercial". The people of Vladivostok do not feel very well-disposed towards the comedian after he attacked the city's modern way of life in one of his performances. What particularly infuriated the Vladivostokians was Zadornov saying that all women in Vladivostok looked like prostitutes. His later "apology", in which he said that what he meant was that prostitutes looked like Vladivostok women, and not the other way round, only added fuel to the fire.

On the other hand, Zadornov still travels all over Russia filling halls. People from every corner of the country still tell him about absurd things they have seen or heard, and his quizzical face is very much part of Russia today. A comic survives when enough people recognize themselves, their own problems, views and issues in his work. While I personally see everything I loathe in his recent work, many in Russia still identify with him.

Language notes:

Задорнов is the writer's real surname, although one could easily think it must be an artistic name, as *"zadorny"* in Russian means "provoking, teasing".

"Как сказал Задорнов..." —"As Zadornov said..."

"Москва сегодня напоминает бомжа, который сделал себе маникюр, педикюр, надел на грязное бельё смокинг и пошёл играть в казино."

"Today's Moscow reminds you of a tramp who has had a manicure and a pedicure, put on a dinner jacket over his dirty underwear and gone out to try his luck at the casino."

"Дружба народов в бывших республиках СССР – это когда все народы объединяются дружить против русских."

"Friendship between peoples of the former republics of the USSR is when they all unite in friendship against the Russians."

"А вот конца света, намеченного на 2012-й, не надо бояться – пускай он страшит Запад. А мы что, конца света не видели?"

"We needn't be scared of the end of the world scheduled for 2012. Let the West be scared. As for us, well, haven't we already seen the end of the world?"

"Россия — государство, победившее разум."

"Russia is a state that has defeated common sense."

"Иногда движение вперёд является результатом пинка сзади."

"Sometimes moving forwards is the result of a kick from behind."

"Россия — великая страна с непредсказуемым прошлым!"

"Russia is a great country with an unpredictable past!"

Mikhail Bulgakov

Михаил Булгаков

One night in the early 1980s, when I was eight or nine years old, my mother made herself comfortable in the kitchen of our flat on the 16th floor of a concrete Soviet block and prepared for a sleepless night alone with a *samizdat* copy of a mysterious book called *The Master and Margarita* that somebody had lent her just for that one night. My curiosity aroused, I asked if I could stay up too, and read over her shoulder, but she told me I wouldn't understand it.

When I read the novel, it had just come out in its first widely-available unabridged official edition in 1989. Mikhail Bulgakov, although almost unpublished during Soviet times, was still a familiar name that aroused great curiosity, and it was with a tremor of anticipation that I first took *The Master and Margarita* in my hands. And it did not disappoint. The passionate and tragic love story, the introduction to Bulgakov's view of biblical events, the mysticism, the struggle between the forces of light and darkness... It was not the satirical aspect of the book that caught my attention back then, but its magical and philosophical qualities, and what attracted my teenage self was the eternal lure of freedom from society, of becoming a witch, hopping onto a broom and flying away (from my parents, mostly): "Invisible, and free!"

The devil visits Moscow using the name of Woland. He brings with him his entourage: a tall slender joker dressed in a checked suit, Koroviev; a huge black cat, Begemot, who can do anything a human being can do and more; the scary angel of death, Azazello; and a delightful bare-breasted vampire, Hella. They arrive in Moscow to tease and taunt, and explore and exploit the particular human weaknesses of the time.

The parallel and intertwined story is the romance of Margarita with a writer. The writer, whom Margarita calls only Master, has been driven to the brink of insanity by the hostile reception to the culmination of his life's work, a novel about Pontius Pilate, and has been robbed of his flat by a false friend. When he ends up in a mental asylum Margarita is ready to do anything to find him, even if it means becoming a witch and playing hostess at Satan's ball.

The third storyline is the encounter between Jesus and Pontius

Pilate, where Bulgakov's version of events deviates significantly from the Gospels – very significantly indeed for someone whose father was a teacher at a seminary in Kiev, and both of whose grandfathers were priests.

The three storylines connect, as the magical world and reality overlap. The story of Pontius Pilate, "the Procurator of Judaea", runs through the novel, and the fabric of the moral and philosophical message of the novel is woven around it. Pontius Pilate becomes besotted with Jesus (in the book Yeshua Ha-Notsri), and wants to set free this crazy philosopher who talks about all people being "good" – until the philosopher gives him his opinion of power as a violent institution, and foresees a future in which a power structure will no longer be necessary. To let him go after saying this would mean putting Pilate's own position in jeopardy, and possibly even worse. Pilate reluctantly condemns Yeshua Ha-Notsri to death.

For Russians of my generation and that of my parents, who grew up in an officially atheist state, the novel – and Bulgakov's interpretation of the relationship between Pontius Pilate and Jesus Christ – was one of our first introductions to the gospel story. Probably my subsequent encounters with the Bible were influenced by first reading *The Master and Margarita*. I cannot help sympathizing with Pontius Pilate, or imagining Christ as a vagabond philosopher whose true teachings we will never know, because his only pupil Matthew the Levite could not quite understand them, nor therefore record them correctly. There are plenty of articles by Russian Orthodox priests lamenting Bulgakov's heresy and its long-lasting influence.

While Bulgakov let his imagination run free in retelling Biblical stories, his depiction of Moscow life in the late 1920s/30s make the book almost a documentary of the time. Of course the novel is a fantasy, but how could you describe life at that time without resorting to fantasy, so surreal was it? The mixture of NEP capitalism (on NEP, see the chapter on *The Twelve Chairs* in this book) and Bolshevik rule, the luxurious lifestyle of the literati, the militant atheism… Bulgakov wrote *The Master and Margarita* between 1929 and 1940, and we can hear in it both the echo of the wild capitalism of NEP and the mass arrests and disappearances of the 1930s – the footsteps on the communal stairway, the sound of the lift in the night, the held breaths behind doors, the hope that it is the neighbour and not oneself who will be arrested and taken away, usually never to be seen again.

Who in 1930s Moscow would not dream of being immune to the oppression of the state machine? To be as nonchalant as Koroviev and Begemot when they hear the footsteps outside the door, carrying on with their card-game, while remarking: "I think someone is coming to arrest us." Reading the novel in the late 1980s, when the USSR was still the USSR but cracks had started to appear in the system, it was heartening to see how it was possible to laugh at the authorities.

To understand what it was like to read *The Master and Margarita* in the Soviet Union, you must remember that mysticism was completely absent from Soviet art. Soviet readers were to some extent familiar with magical realism, as books by Gabriel García Márquez made their way onto their bookshelves. But no magical realism or mysticism could possibly be published in the USSR, where realism (particularly Socialist Realism, which involved the not very realistic glorification of Socialist reality) was the only acceptable style.

All of a sudden we, then teenage Muscovites, had in our hands a novel unlike anything we had ever read before – and it was set not in some remote mythical Macondo, but right here, in prosaic places we had passed though many times, without imagining such things could happen.

This book shifted our view of the world "aesthetically, ethically and politically", as a friend of mine said. Modern Russian writer Victor Pelevin said about *The Master and Margarita*: "The effect of this book was really fantastic. There's an expression 'out of this world'. This book was totally out of the Soviet world. The evil magic of any totalitarian regime is based on its presumed capability to embrace and explain all phenomena, their entire totality, because explanation is control. Hence the term *totalitarian*. So if there's a book that takes you out of this totality of things explained and understood, it liberates you because it breaks the continuity of explanation and thus breaks the spell. It allows you to look in a different direction for a moment, but this moment is enough to understand that everything you saw before was a hallucination... *The Master and Margarita* was exactly this kind of book and it is very hard to explain its subtle effect to anybody who didn't live in the USSR. Solzhenitsyn's books were very anti-Soviet, but they didn't liberate you, they only made you more enslaved since they explained the exact degree to which you were a slave. *The Master and Margarita* didn't even bother to be anti-Soviet, yet reading this book could instantly make you free. It didn't liberate you from some particular old ideas, but rather from the hypnotism of the entire order of things."

So nuanced, so playful and fluid with its treatment of good and evil, Bulgakov's novel was a million miles from Soviet black-and-white, 'friends or enemies' mentality. But it did fall within one Russian literary tradition, feeding the Russian desire to escape from the mundane, from *byt*. The characters showed perennial traits of the Russian psyche, a tendency towards the extreme: selling one's soul to the devil just to be with a loved one, a limitless predisposition to rage, but also a sudden capacity for mercy.

It is hard to say what we actually learnt from the novel, as so many other things were happening around us at the same time. The late '80s and early '90s were the perfect years to read this book, since reading it was very much in tune with those anarchic times when former role models crashed, there were revelations about the USSR's cruel history, gay people appeared on TV, *The Gulag Archipelago* by Solzhenitsyn was published in Russia... The history exam had to be cancelled the year I took my exams for the university, because nobody knew how, in the light of new revelations, to evaluate students' knowledge. What had once been presented as solid fact had suddenly melted away. All things, even the most incredible things, were possible. And *The Master and Margarita* was more evidence of that.

Reading *The Master and Margarita* was certainly part of "being there" rather than "being square" – as well as speaking languages, having foreign friends, listening to *The Doors* (yes, in the early '90s). Russian boys took female foreign students for walks at Patriarch's Ponds just as the sun was setting, whispering into their unsuspecting ears quotes from the novel, such as "Never talk to strangers!" (the title of the first chapter in the book).

❀❀❀

Bulgakov himself insisted that he was primarily a satirist. But I still find it difficult to read *The Master and Margarita* as a mainly satirical novel; nor is it very clear this is what it was meant to be – after all, when the researcher into Soviet satire of the 1920s, Abram Vulis (who was instrumental in getting the novel published for the first time in 1966), contacted Bulgakov's widow Yelena, asking her about a rumoured manuscript of the satirical novel by Bulgakov he had heard about, she answered it was not satirical but philosophical. Of course, satire is there, aimed at the literary circles of the time, at Soviet reality and at militant atheism. The book is certainly full of irony. But there is something very dark and pessimistic that permeates this novel, and if we tend to think that a satirical writer is someone who wants to change things by revealing their ridiculous side, in Bulgakov's writing no change is possible unless you reject reality completely – either by siding with the forces of darkness, or by going insane. The only "normal" and decent place in the whole of late '20s-early '30s Moscow is the lunatic asylum, where the sheets are white, the baths are luxurious, the view is calm and the staff are kind, despite Bulgakov's hero calling it on more than one occasion *dom skorbi* – "the house of sorrow" – a rarely used Russian expression for a mental institution.

You can just imagine Bulgakov, unable to have his works published, persecuted by critics (he wrote in his "Letter to the Government of the USSR" in 1930 that in the preceding 10 years of reviews of his work, 3 were positive, 298 hostile), asking repeatedly and unsuccessfully to be allowed to leave the USSR – writing this novel, dreaming of freedom from his surroundings, and nurturing dreams of sweet revenge on the Moscow literary world. When Bulgakov depicts Moscow writers' lavish lifestyle it is clear he is on the outside, and when he describes Margarita's revenge on the Master's critics, when she creates havoc in the flats of her lover's opponents, you can feel the writer's own glee.

Bulgakov hated the flat at 50 Bolshaya Sadovaya where he lived in the mid-1920s, and which in his novel is occupied by Woland and his intimates. This was a communal flat– that is, a large apartment, formerly the property of a well-off family, which after the revolution had been divided into many rooms with all the inhabitants using the same kitchen and bathroom. Bulgakov's first wife Tatiana recalled never having a moment's peace, while the numerous flatmates would be "making homemade vodka, squabbling and often scuffling with one another". A prostitute, Dusya, lived next door, and sometimes the Bulgakovs would get a knock on the door in the middle of the night and would have to direct the visitor to her room.

Particularly troublesome was the terrible Annushka. Bulgakov wrote in 1923 in his diary: "Today for the first time the communal heating has been switched on. I spent the whole evening insulating the windows. The first day of having the heating on was marked by the famous Annushka leaving the window in the kitchen wide open the whole night. I positively don't know what to do with the bastards who live in this flat."

Annushka, also known by the nickname *Chumá* – The Plague – is of course a minor character in *The Master and Margarita*, minor but fatal: she is the one who spills the sunflower oil near the tram crossing, making Berlioz, the chairman of the writers' union, slip and get his head cut off by a tram, just as had been predicted a few minutes before by the mysterious stranger he met at Patriarch's Ponds.

During our aimless wanderings round Moscow, my best friend and I would sometimes drop by Bulgakov's flat, a cult place for hippies. The door to the flat was always shut, but the landing walls were absolutely covered with paintings of various degrees of proficiency of characters and scenes from *The Master and Margarita*, quotations from the novel, and lyrics from the Beatles and Jim Morrison.

The flat has been turned into a Bulgakov museum, and even though the walls get cleaned from time to time, new paintings keep appearing. Going up that stairway, you can still see the black-haired witch on a broom, a big black cat holding a fork with a gherkin and Pontius Pilate "in a white cape with blood-red lining".

Moscow has obviously changed tremendously from the '30s. The descriptions of the city in the novel are rather schematic, and those who know the place can fill in the details. Those of us who know the city of the late twentieth and early twenty-first centuries can imagine what the Master saw as he said goodbye to the city from Sparrow Hills. The Hills still give a good view of Moscow, but what is left of those years? It's easier to imagine a cul-de-sac near the Arbat, somewhere in the maze of those little streets that were left relatively untouched, and a basement flat hidden in a yard, with a window on which Margarita liked to playfully tap with the toe of her shoe. Patriarch's Ponds, a park in central Moscow with a small lake and shaded alleys, still provide Muscovites with relief from heat in the summer, and in the winter they are full of children skating on the frozen surface of the pond or sliding on sledges or pieces of cardboard down the icy banks.

When Bulgakov read the novel to his friends in 1939, the fruit of more than 10 years' labour, they knew immediately the novel could not possibly be published, and advised him against even trying to get it published. The novel was first published in 1966, 26 years after Bulgakov's death and during the brief period of hope and (relative) freedom that came to be known as Khrushchev's "thaw". It came out in *Moskva* magazine in an abridged version, in which the twelve per cent of the text considered most dangerous was removed by the editors. However, the redacted parts made their way into the *samizdat* version and were passed around. In 1973 the first complete version of the novel was published in a small print-run, and some of the lucky people who owned the book were kind enough to make facsimile copies and pass them around. Then finally in 1989 the novel came out in a large print run, and in its unabridged version.

There were various Soviet-era writers who were tragically incapable of accepting Soviet reality or adapting their life or their writing to it, but Mikhail Bulgakov was a particular misfit. He himself knew it very well, writing in his diary: "In moments of sickness and loneliness I give myself up to sad and envious thoughts. I bitterly regret giving up medicine and condemning myself to this uncertain existence. But God knows the only reason for this was my love for literature. Literature now is a difficult business. With my views reflected in my writing whether or not I want them to be, it is hard to get published, and to live".

You need only read this paragraph from another of Bulgakov's novels, *The White Guard*, to feel the writer's nostalgia for pre-revolutionary times: "In house number 13 on Alekseyevsky Rise, the stove covered with ceramic tiles had warmed and brought up little Yelena, the older Alexei and tiny Nikolka. ...the clock chimed a gavotte, and in late December there was the smell of fir trees, with multicoloured paraffin burning on the green branches... Those stove tiles, the furniture upholstered with old red velvet, the beds with shiny finials, well-rubbed carpets, motley-crimson, with a falcon on tsar Alexei Mikhailovich's hand, with Louis XIV lounging on the bank of a silky lake in a garden paradise, Turkish rugs with odd curls against the Oriental background that loomed before Nikolka's eyes in the delirium of the scarlet fever, the bronze shaded lamp, the best bookcases in the world, smelling of mysterious antique chocolate, with Natasha Rostov, *The Captain's Daughter*, the gilded cups, the silver, the portraits, the curtains..."

The White Guard is an exquisitely subtle, elegant and atmospheric novel set in Bulgakov's native Kiev in the winter of 1918. *Gorod* – the

City, as Kiev is referred to in the novel – is in snowy hibernation, and a fragile, deceptive state of peace. It is being governed by the newly formed Ukrainian government (Hetmanate) supported by the German military. But from the suburbs the sounds of artillery are heard and rumours are flying around the city. Simon Petlura, the Ukrainian ultra-nationalist whose troops hunt down and kill former Russian army officers, is somewhere nearby. But what is more disturbing, and what everyone is dreading, is the arrival of the Red Army. The Turbin siblings, Alexei the military doctor, Yelena and the cadet Nikolka hold onto their fragile world around the hot white-and-blue ceramic tiled stove, behind the closed "cream-coloured" curtains.

Reading any of Bulgakov's books, it's obvious he was unpublishable. Take *A Dog's Heart* (*Собачье сердце*), his novel set in the years immediately after the revolution, about Professor Preobrazhensky's experiment in transplanting a human pituitary gland and testicles to a stray dog. The operation turns the dog into a human being of sorts. This new half-beast, half-man combines some dog-like habits with the personality of his human donor, the balalaika-playing felon Klim Chugunkin. Acquiring the surname of Sharikov (from Sharik, a very popular Russian name for a dog, meaning "ball"), the beast gets on surprisingly well in Soviet society (getting a job exterminating stray cats), and gets a warm welcome and political guidance from the local commissar Shvonder. *A Dog's Heart* is a bitter satire on the creation of the new Soviet man, *homo sovieticus*, whose political views are basic: "Take everything, and divide it between everyone!"

The refined professor Preobrazhensky, a gourmet and opera lover, felt quite immune from the revolutionary changes before he created Sharikov. Famous for his "rejuvenation" operations and counting among his clients some high governmental officials, he has managed to keep his possessions and his apartment of seven rooms. He is also not restrained in his speech, confessing that he does not like the proletariat and discussing in very unequivocal terms what he thinks about the so called *разруха* (*razrukha*) – "ruin", the word used for the chaos and shortages of the post-revolutionary period. Accompanied by the communal revolutionary choir from the flat below, he tells his assistant Bormenthal off for using this word to excuse the state of things:

"This is a mirage, a smoke, fiction… What is this 'ruin'? An old woman with a crutch? A witch who has shuttered all the windows and extinguished all the lights? She does not exist! What do you mean when you use this word?... This is what it is: if instead of operating every evening I have choir-singing in my apartment, it will come to ruin. If when I go to the bathroom I start – if you would please excuse me – missing the toilet while urinating, and Zina and Darya Petrovna start doing the same thing, the bathroom will go to ruin. So 'ruin' is not in the closet, it is in people's heads."

You can imagine Bulgakov agreeing with nearly everything Preobrazhnesky says. Still Preobrazhensky, whose surname comes from преображение (*preobrazhenie*) – "transfiguration" – is a bit of a decadent figure with his comfortable life derived from cashing in on people's vanity. In his Faustian striving to break through the limits of knowledge, the old professor oversteps the line. "Professor Preobrazhensky, you are a creator!" exclaims doctor Bormenthal as he watches the dog slowly acquire human form. But interfering in the Creator's business costs the professor dear, as he himself admits: "Here doctor, this is what happens when a scientist, instead of following nature tentatively and closely, forces the issue and raises the curtain: here he is, Sharikov..." The Creator has accidentally given birth to a new creature, someone who plays the balalaika while singing obscene rhymes, and drinks too much vodka while chasing crazily after cats and using his teeth to pick out fleas.

As Sharikov gets ahead in the Soviet world the professor's confidence fades and his health quickly deteriorates. Life in the flat becomes more and more unbearable, and Dr Bormenthal, Professor Preobrazhensky's loyal disciple, begins to think about murder.

In the late 1980s, when the novel became widely known – and was made into an excellent film as well as being staged by several theatres – the questions of Evolution versus Revolution, or whether history should be forced or allowed to evolve slowly in its own direction, were passionately discussed in the press and in people's kitchens. Bulgakov's view was very clear: "My beloved Great Evolution," he wrote in 1930 in his 'Letter to The Government of the USSR'. In that same letter he also wrote, with a courage perhaps born of desperation: "The struggle against censorship, in any form and under any government, is my duty as a writer, as is calling for freedom of the press. I am a fervent supporter of this freedom, and believe that for any writer to suggest it is not necessary would be like a fish publicly announcing it has no need of water."

Was it this courage and disarming honesty that ultimately saved Bulgakov from physical reprisals at a time when to die in your own bed was an unlikely prospect for any out-of-favour public figure? As it was, Bulgakov died of a chronic illness at home at the age of 48, having asked his third wife Yelena to look after the manuscript he had worked on during the last 12 years of his life: *The Master and Margarita*. Yelena Bulgakova tidied up the manuscript, making the author's latest corrections, and guarded it until the abridged version could be published in 1966. "Manuscripts don't burn" is probably the most famous phrase from the novel, which was much quoted to proclaim the defiant survival of art against repression. For Bulgakov at least, who once threw the first draft of his novel into a fire in a moment of despair, just like the Master, his line has come true.

Bulgakov is often named by Russians of different generations as one of their favourite writers, and *The Master and Margarita* is many people's desert island book – the book they would take with them if they were only allowed one choice. Just as in the West, most Russians first read *The Master and Margarita* as teenagers, dipping their toes into philosophical questions, and liking books that read as though they were written on acid. But this is a book that many people return to as adults. You can always find something new there. Bulgakov, for Russians, combines the classics and the modern, and Russians prefer classics to wasting their time reading something new that may or may not be good. At the same time, Bulgakov's style is modern, and although life has changed since the 1930s, many things are still recognizable. Bulgakov has quite an impressionistic way of describing characters, but each character in the book, however small, is an archetype. Russians find it easy to complete these images in their imagination and they see them as familiar, true and funny.

I am one of those rare Russians who, while I love Bulgakov, do not think *The Master and Margarita* is his best or most subtle novel. His humour, his imagery, his attention to detail, his simple and at the same time mesmerizing style are better seen in *The White Guard* or *A Dog's Heart*. But the success of "magical realism" has made *The Master and Margarita* Bulgakov's best-known book; it fulfils the need to believe in miracles and the ultimate victory of justice, a need that is perhaps even stronger in Russia than in many other places.

Language notes:

From *The Master and Margarita:*

"Кирпич ни с того ни с сего... никому и никогда на голову не свалится." – "A brick never falls on anyone's head for no reason at all." – This is what Woland says to Berlioz while they are arguing, on a bench in Patriarch's Ponds, whether man is master of his own destiny.

"Обыкновенные люди... в общем, напоминают прежних... квартирный вопрос только испортил их" – "They are normal people... all in all, they are as they always were... it's just that the housing shortage has corrupted them." – This is what Woland has to say about Muscovites.

"Рукописи не горят" – "Manuscripts don't burn" – Woland says, when he uses his magic to present the Master with the manuscript of his novel about Pontius Pilate that the writer had himself burned in the stove. This has been used a lot, when talking about Bulgakov and other writers' works surviving through Soviet times.

"Не шалю, никого не трогаю, починяю примус..." – "I am not up to anything, I'm not bothering anyone, I'm just repairing the Primus ..." – The mischievous cat Begemot is pretending to be ordinary – though the sight of a huge black talking cat repairing a Primus stove is perhaps enough to send anyone into a state of panic.

"Вторая свежесть – вот что вздор! Свежесть бывает только одна – первая, она же и последняя. А если осетрина второй свежести, то это означает, что она тухлая!" – "Second freshness is rubbish! There is only one degree of freshness – the first, which is also the last. If the sturgeon is of the 'second freshness', it is off!" – This refers to the popular Soviet expression "second freshness" – not quite fresh.

"Аннушка уже пролила масло" – "Annushka has already spilled the oil" – A train of events has been set in motion...

From *A Heart of a Dog*:

"Шариков" – Sharikov: the name of the man made from a dog has come to be used extensively to point out someone's complete lack of culture and civilized behaviour (can also be used in plural – "шариковы").

"Если вы заботитесь о своем пищеварении... не читайте до обеда советских газет" – "If you care about your digestion... do not read Soviet newspapers before lunch" – the advice of Professor Preobrazhensky.

THE PROSTOKVASHINO THREE

ТРОЕ ИЗ ПРОСТОКВАШИНО

A young Russian recently wrote on Twitter that when he eats a *buterbrod*, a Russian open sandwich which is really a piece of bread with something, possibly sausage, on top, he turns it upside-down so that the sausage touches his tongue first and not the bread – just because it was once recommended in one famous animated cartoon by one famous cat.

The cat in question is, of course, Cat Matroskin, a protagonist of the animated film *The Prostokvashino Three* that appeared in 1978. It was followed shortly by two more episodes, *Holidays in Prostokvashino* and *Winter in Prostokvashino*, and the three films have been repeated constantly on children's TV shows ever since. Not only children but adults too would drop whatever they were doing to settle in front of the screen at the first notes of the opening theme, enjoying the humour of these cartoons and their take on familiar subjects, such as relationships between parents and children, the differences between country and city life, and the bickering between cats and dogs.

In this cartoon a young boy from a big city, possibly Moscow, nicknamed Uncle Fyodor for his precocious common sense, meets a stray cat while going downstairs in his apartment block. The boy is munching on a sandwich, and the cat called Matroskin ("фамилие такое" – "this is my family name", he likes to explain, using an unusual neuter gender of "familiye" instead of the correct "familiya") strikes up a conversation with him, telling him how to improve his sandwich-eating technique (by turning it upside down so that the sausage touches his tongue first – the sandwich will taste much better). The cat also hints he has nowhere to live and asks Uncle Fyodor if up in his flat he has any more "incorrect" sandwiches.

The boy invites Matroskin to his flat, but when his parents arrive, his mother is most unimpressed. The father tries to chip in on the cat's behalf, but is given an ultimatum by the mother: "Choose, the cat or me!" To give *papa* credit he tries to be fair, and looks at the cat and back at his wife a few times, before finally saying to his wife: "Well, I am choosing you. I've known you for a long time, and this is the first time that I've seen this cat."

So Uncle Fyodor, very upset that his parents won't let him keep a pet, decides to run away from home with Cat Matroskin and live in a village. When they arrive in the village of Prostokvashino (Buttermilk), they are met by a stray dog, Sharik, who shows them an abandoned house. The three set up home there, under the suspicious eyes of a local postman, Pechkin.

The Prostokvashino series has three episodes: *The Prostokvashino Three*, *Holidays in Prostokvashino* (where Uncle Fyodor runs off to see his animal friends in the village, while his parents travel to a seaside resort where his mum can show off her new dresses) and *Winter in Prostokvashino* (where Sharik and Matroskin have serious arguments on New Year's Eve, but are reunited again by the arrival of Uncle Fyodor).

The characters of the Prostokvashino cartoons have been very much part of the life of children (and their parents) in Russia from the late 1970s until today.

Uncle Fyodor is a very independent and mature boy who likes animals. He tends to wear slightly hippyish trousers and his hair-style varies wildly across the three episodes. He is an unquestionable authority for Sharik and Matroskin, and they rely on him to make wise decisions, such as, for example, looking for hidden treasure in order to get the money to buy a cow (an undertaking in which, sure enough, they immediately succeed). Uncle Fyodor is always keen to spend his holidays in Prostokvashino with his animal friends, but his mother usually has other things in mind...

Uncle Fyodor's mum is a rather attractive though somewhat highly strung woman – authoritarian and capricious, but kind-hearted. Breaking gender stereotypes obviously was not on the agenda of 1970s Soviet cartoon-makers. Uncle Fyodor's mum always protests when the other family members suggest spending their holiday in the village, although she loves Prostokvashino really. She just keeps forgetting just quite how much she likes it. But she also keeps rediscovering it, in every episode.

Uncle Fyodor's dad is a relaxed bearded chap who is always wearing a sweater, looking like a slightly scruffy Russian physics professor of the 1960s or '70s. He would like the house to be chaotic and jolly, full of children and animals, but is restrained by his wife.

Dog Sharik is a pretty typical street dog, a bit simple, slightly silly and desperate to be part of a pack. He is constantly being mocked by the cat and is always getting into ridiculous situations, such as almost drowning in a lake when he refuses to let go of a rifle, or buying some light running shoes in the middle of a Russian winter when Matroskin sends him to buy some felt boots.

But it is Cat Matroskin who is constantly voted the coolest of the characters on the *Prostokvashino* fan websites. He is a stripy cat whose grandparents lived on sailing ships, hence his sea-related name Matroskin, coming from *матрос* (*matros*), a sailor. He himself has lived in different places and thinks of himself as being an old hand at many things. He is down-to-earth, pragmatic, very careful with money and possesses a wry, even slightly sarcastic, sense of humour, directed mostly at the dog.

Matroskin is voiced by the inimitable Oleg Tabakov, a theatre and cinema star and director. Tabakov became so associated with this character, despite the dozens of other parts he has played in a career that spans 50 years, he is sometimes given presents of paintings in which he very much resembles the cat and wears a sailor's cap.

Postman Pechkin is not a very pleasant character, a slightly malicious but amusing village postman. He is nosy and a bit of a jobsworth. But of course without him this cartoon would not be the same, as he creates some of the funniest moments.

And then there is a little bird, a Jackdaw, who is taught to say "Kto tam?" – "Who's there?" every time anyone knocks on the door, and repeats some of Postman Pechkin phrases, to everyone's amusement.

★★★

When children all over the USSR made themselves comfortable in front of the screen in the evening (well, those children who had a TV set in the house), they would look forward to their favourite programme, *Goodnight, Little Ones! – Спокойной ночи, малыши!* Every night they would be greeted by a presenter – usually female – and puppets: rebellious piggy Khryusha, teacher's pet rabbit Stepashka and the obedient and serious dog Filya. The puppets would usually have some instructive conversation with the presenter (about how to cross the road properly, for example), and afterwards an animated cartoon would be shown. The film would not be announced in advance, and it was always a pleasant surprise when a particular cartoon favourite appeared, like one of the three *Prostokvashino* episodes.

Every Russian knows by heart, and can sing, the closing song of the *Good Night, Little Ones!* programme. (If you meet a Russian who doesn't, he is definitely a Western spy.) This is how it goes:

Спят усталые игрушки, книжки спят.
Одеяла и подушки ждут ребят.
Даже сказка спать ложится,
Чтобы ночью нам присниться,
Ты ей пожелай
Баю-бай.

"The tired toys are sleeping, and the books are sleeping too.
The blankets and pillows are waiting for the kids.
Even the fairy tale is going to sleep,
So that it can appear in our dreams.
Wish it goodnight."

After first appearing in 1964, *Good Night, Little Ones!* carried on through Soviet and post-Soviet times, trying to make Russian children more like obedient Stepashka and Filya, and less like the rebellious Khrusha. The 1970s was, of course, when television entered most Soviet households for the first time and started to perform the role of storyteller and mythologizer for children and adults alike. It was interesting for me to read an article by Yelena Prokhorova about the programme, in which she shows how so many TV symbols of the 1970s are used by the advertising industry now, exploiting myths of the "stability" of Soviet times and the longing of a large part of the population for this stability. The fact that the programme has lasted for 40 years is emphasized by its team, as well as by the advertising industry, to underline the unity of cultural values now and during Soviet times, the "uninterrupted cultural transmission", in Prokhorova's words, all the way through to the new Russia. The idea of the natural and uninterrupted development of modern Russia from the USSR, as in preserving the "greatness" and "achievements" of the Soviet times, is very much part of the modern Russian government's ideology. The (often somewhat modified) memories of the Soviet past, in which jobs were for life, holidays were inexpensive and healthcare free, fill a vacuum in the new Russian middle class's value system. Meanwhile, the mass media is putting the little ones and their parents to sleep, as it has increasingly been doing all over the world…

Good Night, Little Ones! is now presented, among others, by Oksana Fyodorova, Miss Universe 2002 and a reserve police major. This change of presenters in the most symbolic children's programme reflects the overall situation in a country where the security services are running the government. I am sure the moral lessons are conveyed to the children even more efficiently.

Hardly of the same moral standing is a new Russian reality show, whose name mimics the name of the children's programme: *Спокойной ночи, мужики!* – *Goodnight, Lads!*

I know it is a bit of a digression, but I just have to relay to you its concept, it is so perfectly post-Soviet Russia, flamboyant and dynamic, immoral, bizarre and tawdry. In this TV game, three straight couples (married or unmarried) are locked in a studio setting together with one unattached girl and a "subject". Each of the four girls is out there to seduce the subject and convince him that she is the one who is unattached. The subject has to decide which of the girls is single. Meanwhile, the partners of the three girls have a chance to watch on video all the advances their better halves are making to a stranger. Their remarks are heard on TV, and often have to be interrupted by bleeps. If any of the men thinks his partner has gone too far, he can press the stop button… But then he and his girlfriend or wife are kicked out of the game and lose their chance to win the prize of 150,000 roubles, equivalent to around £3,300. The participants are usually from not-very-wealthy areas in Russia, and the competition runs hot. If the protagonist guesses correctly who the unattached girl is, he and the girl share the prize. If he makes a mistake, the girl who convinced him she is single and her partner get the prize.

★★★

But let us come back to *Prostokvashino*, and why it became such an important cultural signifier of pre-*perestroika* Russia. Why indeed? I am not quite sure myself. But here is an opinion from researcher Yelena Baraban, who also thinks it is rather unfair that such a popular film is often not included in studies of Soviet animation.

According to Baraban, the tone of this film fitted very well with the mood of that part of Soviet society that in the 1970s, disillusioned both with official ideology and with attempts to fight it, turned their backs on social and communal life and put all their energy into creating their own private paradise, usually at their *dachas*. They put their efforts and imagination into disproving Lenin's postulate that "one cannot live in society and be free from society", participating in society as little as was possibly compatible with official requirements and retreating into their own world of friends, family, country hikes, apples and cucumbers.

This was definitely the mood I remember at our obligatory Komsomol (Young Communists) meetings at school: apart from the very few ardently active members, most of us wanted this to be over with and to go home and do more interesting things. You can also see people's cynical attitude towards Soviet ideology and its values in the apparently apolitical films of Eldar Ryazanov.

In *The Prostokvashino Three* society virtually does not exist – although it is partly represented by Postman Pechkin, the nosy officious individual whose appearance is always sudden and never welcome. Pechkin thinks he has the right to intrude into people's (and animals') private lives, he is greedy and not very bright. He is a bit of a busybody, who takes pleasure in trying to make sure nobody has broken any rules. He likes to torment our protagonists with bureaucratic impediments. In the end Uncle Fyodor and the others learn to deal with Pechkin, although there remains an understanding that he can never be fully trusted – as is the case with the world outside the Prostokvashino paradise. Pechkin's annoying incursions into our protagonists' idyllic existence remind us that the imperfect world does exist somewhere far far away from the Prostokvashino house, in which the samovar is always on and the cow gives so much milk that they don't know what to do with it.

Though not always so delightfully escapist, many Soviet-made cartoons are still watched and enjoyed by Russian children.

For example, *Ну, погоди!* – *Just You Wait!* where Wolf and Rabbit try to outwit each other much in the same way as Tom and Jerry, but in less violent fashion. In one of them Rabbit dresses as Father Frost, and Wolf has to dress as a Snow maiden just to get on the stage and closer to his prey...

Or how about *Падал прошлогодний снег* – *Last Year's Snow Was Falling*. This tale of a slightly dim-witted village man being sent to the woods by his wife to get a Christmas tree and encountering all sorts of magic on his way is a fine absurdist story, combining motifs from various Russian folktales, and made even more surreal by the plasticine animation, where anything can suddenly turn into something else.

Крошка енот – *Tiny Raccoon* – is another that every Russian child has seen. It is a story about a little raccoon who wants to prove he is big enough to get some sugarcane from the pond, at night, all on his own, and encounters in the mirror of the pond a very aggressive looking little raccoon... But when his mother advises he smiles to the stranger, the raccoon from the pond smiles back.

And of course, the Russian *Winnie-the-Pooh (Винни-Пух)* is just a masterpiece. He is rather rounder than his Disney counterpart, and very chirpy indeed. Every Russian child and adult knows his songs by heart.

There are many animated cartoons that, like *The Prostokvashino Three*, are based on children's stories by Eduard Uspensky – like those about Cheburashka, an otherworldly creature who looks a bit like a lemur with big round eyes and big ears. His friend is a good-natured crocodile, Gena, and his enemy is Old Shapoklyak, a nasty thin old lady who likes to make trouble and who, as Uspensky remarked rather ungallantly, was based on his first wife.

After *perestroika*, the stream of subsidy to the animation industry shrank dramatically, and Russian animation hit hard times. Now it also has to compete in an unequal battle with Disney. But the old Soviet cartoons are still watched, both in Russia and outside: non-Russian schoolfriends of Russians abroad seem to be fascinated by the adventures of Uncle Fyodor and his friends, even without understanding the dialogue. Maybe the dream of running away into a parent-free paradise full of dogs and cats is universal.

Language notes:

"Неправильно ты, дядя Фёдор, бутерброд ешь. Ты его колбасой кверху держишь, а надо колбасой на язык класть, мм... Так вкуснее получится." At the very beginning of the film Matroskin, seeing Uncle Fyodor coming downstairs in the block of flats, strikes up a conversation with him, saying: "Uncle Fyodor, you are eating your sandwich wrong. You've got the sausage on top, but you need to put the sausage on your tongue, mmm... Then it tastes better."

"Кот Матроскин меня зовут. Это фамилие такое." – Cat Matroskin is very proud of his surname, the comical effect is achieved by him using a grammatically incorrect neuter form "familiye" instead of the feminine "familiya" : "My name is Cat Matroskin. This is my surname."

"Я ничей, я сам по себе мальчик — свой собственный." – Postman Pechkin is trying to find out where the newcomers are from, and what a boy is doing on his own in a village with a dog and a cat. To his question "Whose child are you?" Uncle Fyodor replies: "Nobody's – I am my own boy."

"Мясо лучше в магазине покупать." – "Почему?" – "Там костей больше." This dialogue almost didn't get past the censor. Sharik and Matroskin are talking about where to buy meat, in a shop or at the market, with Sharik saying: "It's better to buy meat in a shop," and to Matroskin's "Why?" he explains: "It has more bones" – rather a pointed comment about the quality of meat in Soviet shops. The author of the story, Uspensky, somehow managed to convince the censor to let it through.

"Кто там?" – "Это я, почтальон Печкин, принёс заметку про вашего мальчика." – "Who's there?" the little Jackdaw asks – "It's me, Postman Pechkin, I brought a newspaper cutting about your boy" – this is a universally-recognized reference: answering "Postman Pechkin" to the question "Who's there?" is sure to raise a smile with your Russian friends.

"Подумаешь! Я ещё и вышивать могу, и на машинке — тоже…" – Uncle Fyodor's mum is warming to Cat Matroskin, and he is trying to impress her even further: "That's nothing… I can also do embroidery, and use a sewing machine…"

"Вон он. С охоты возвращается. Охотничек. Наверно, добычу тащит." Matroskin is watching from a distance a beaver dragging along Sharik, whom he has saved from drowning, and comments: "Here he comes from the hunt. A heck of a hunter. Probably bringing some prey."

"Я вам посылку принёс, только я вам её не отдам, потому как у вас документов нету." Postman Pechkin is a bit of a jobsworth: "I brought you a parcel, but I am not going to give it to you, because you have no documents." To which Matroskin answers, indignantly: "Усы, лапы, хвост — вот мои документы!" – "Whiskers, paws, tail – those are my documents!"

"На дворе конец двадцатого века…" – "Да!" - "… а у нас одна пара валенок на двоих." In the middle of winter, Postman Pechkin is visiting Sharik and Matroskin. The two animals are not talking to each other. Matroskin comments: "Out there it is the end of the twentieth century…" The little Jackdraw confirms: "Yes!" – "And we have just one pair of felt boots between the two of us." Postman Pechkin suggests Matroskin complains to Sharik, but as the two are not talking, the postman suggests the cat send a telegram, which he then promptly delivers across the room to the dog. As the only forms left are special occasion telegram forms, the cat is supposed to first congratulate Sharik on something. Matroskin writes: "Поздравляю тебя, Шарик, ты балбес!" - "Congratulations, Sharik, you are a moron!"

Sharik responds by making a drawing on the wall of the stove. The drawing resembles a wigwam. When asked to explain, he says it is "figvam", "a national Indian house". "Фига" is a gesture in which you make a fist, placing your thumb between you index and middle finger. In Russia (unlike in some other countries) it is a bit of a childish gesture, which is not particularly rude, and signifies "you are not getting anything out of me"! "Фиг вам" – "a figa to you", makes a funny play on words with wigwam.

HEDGEHOG IN THE MIST

ЁЖИК В ТУМАНЕ

It's always a pleasure (though it can be embarrassing, too) to watch as an adult a film or cartoon you used to like as a child. It can also be rewarding to return to cartoons created ostensibly for children, but more suitable for adult sensibilities, which you did not particularly like or appreciate as a child. For me, the animated film *Hedgehog in the Mist*, made in 1975 by Yuri Norstein, is one such. Watching it again now, it is interesting to see how different it is from computer-generated animation. It is also curious to stop and look closely at a work whose imagery is part of my memory, even though I was never a real fan.

Often, just before it gets dark, little Hedgehog sets off to visit his friend Bear Cub. Bear Cub lights the samovar, Hedgehog brings a jar of jam, and together they sit on the porch of Bear Cub's house, drink tea, eat jam and count stars. The stars on the left of the chimney are Hedgehog's, and the ones on the right belong to Bear Cub.

One evening Hedgehog, as usual, sets off for Bear Cub's house. He is slightly absent-minded, mumbling to himself in anticipation of a pleasant evening with his friend. He is thinking what he will say to Bear Cub, and what Bear Cub will reply... Suddenly, he sees a valley covered with mist, and a white horse right at the bottom. He wonders if the horse will drown in the mist if it lies down to sleep. To find out what it's like down there, he wanders into the misty valley.

There is a scary-looking Owl who seems to be pursuing the Hedgehog without his realizing. A dry leaf falls down, swirling, and frightens him. In the dreamy reality of twilight, everything in the forest is mysterious and beautiful. The real and the imaginary, the shadows and the outlines mix. The white horse is drowning in the white mist. One minute everything is peaceful and beautiful, the next minute it is full of the unknown and terrifying. The shimmering quality of the landscape in the movie is Norstein's trademark, playing with light and shade.

Every little detail in this film is thought through: the movement of a swirling leaf; the Hedgehog's surprised face, his nose pointing upwards, his eyes wide open in astonishment at the wonders of the world around him; his little bundle, in which he is carrying a jar of raspberry jam – or rather *varenye*, a fruit preserve – to his friend Bear Cub. The agile midges dancing in the twilit air. The call of Bear Cub, worried that his friend has not yet arrived, ringing through the mist: *"Yo-o-o-zhik!"* – *"Little He-e-edgehog!"*

Having almost lost the jar of raspberry jam, and narrowly escaped drowning in the river, thanks to the kindness of a mysterious stranger – a big fish – Hedgehog finally arrives at the worried Bear Cub's house. He looks stunned after his adventures. Bear Cub is worried. He has lit the samovar, using juniper twigs that give the tea a special smoky flavour. He has been looking forward to his raspberry jam. But more than anything he is happy that his friend is safe: "Who will count the stars, if you aren't here?" he exclaims. As they prepare to drink their tea, Bear Cub babbling away with joy, Hedgehog looks slightly absent. He is thinking about the Horse. How is she out there, in the mist?

Hedgehog in the Mist is based on a tale by Sergei Kozlov, who wrote a set of charming children's stories about a group of animals – a Hedgehog, a Bear Cub, a Hare, an Owl, and others who all live in the same wood. There is also an Ant, who is the only animal in the wood that does any work – and also encourages others to do the same: "Работать надо каждый день, каждый день, каждый день!" – "You must work every day, every day, every day!" But no one seems to be convinced working is the best way to spend one's time, certainly not Little Hedgehog and his friend Bear Cub. They seem to spend their time drinking tea and admiring the changing landscapes of the forest, having philosophical (if childish) conversations. This pattern is sometimes broken when they have to be heroic, for example when Hedgehog gets caught in a trap, and Bear Cub has to rescue him and feed him with mushroom soup to make him recover quickly. But, most of the time, the animals pass the time pleasantly, for example playing the game of closing their eyes while the sun is setting, and opening them to see the transformed landscape, and the hill and the valleys changing colour.

It does remind me of my own long summer holidays in the tiny Ukrainian town of Tulchin. We would arrive there in mid-June, after a day and a half's train journey. The house was empty during the winter, and we first of all had to chase away the spiders that had made it their home, wash the cutlery and unpack all the lace curtains and tablecloths my grandmother insisted on always taking with her wherever she went. The folding beds would be put up for me and my aunt, while my grandmother would get the ancient iron bed. And then... a heavenly two months lazing on the folding bed with a library book, with a plateful of fruit from the daily visit to a local market. The scrumptious, aromatic, bursting-with-flavour Ukrainian fruit – nothing has ever tasted like that since. Endless games of chess. Walking in the town park until it got dark and the bats appeared. The open-air cinema with cartoons...

❈❈❈

This cartoon also makes me think of dreams and dreaminess, and the role they play in the life of the Russians. "A blue tit in your hand is better than a crane in the sky," says the Russian proverb, but many Russians believe just the opposite, preferring a good dream to the drudgery of reality. Russian culture has a lot of imaginative tendencies; Russians also have to deal with the constant restrictions imposed by a succession of oppressive governments. That makes some Russians, at least the so-called intelligentsia, go into the state that a child often goes into when she is being bullied or bored – the world of the imagination. Escapism is of course common to everyone, with drugs and alcohol often called upon for assistance. But it seems to me that while in the West many artists, particularly rock stars, get stuck in their teenage years, in Russia creative people get stuck in their childhood. Teenagers are rebellious, and are constantly trying to challenge their parents. In a place where these attempts to challenge tend to be crushed with disproportionate brutality, like Russia, they retreat further back into childhood, and stay there.

I am thinking in this context about the generation that Russian rock legend Boris Grebeshchikov called in his song "the generation of yard-keepers and security guards". In 1961 a decree was passed by the Soviet government "On intensifying the fight against individuals avoiding socially-useful labour and conducting a parasitic anti-social way of life". In the USSR working was not only a right, it was an obligation. Writing poetry or painting while not being a member of the writers' or artists' union would not be considered work, and so the anti-establishment artists who did not belong to the proper regulatory body were in constant danger of being arrested as "parasites". The poet Joseph Brodsky was famously charged with "idleness" (*тунеядство*) in 1964 and sent to the countryside to do forced labour.

Many artists who were not part of the establishment, and even scientists who lost their jobs because of disagreements with their superiors, found themselves in a position where they had to find unqualified jobs so as not to be arrested for "idleness" – jobs such as yard keepers, security guards in warehouses, lift operators... These jobs did not take too much of their time, and allowed them to do what they wanted. They could also keep dreaming their dreams while at work, undisturbed... Just like Little Hedgehog and Bear Cub. Let the unimaginative Ant do "socially useful" work.

Many escaped into their dreams, but some also escaped to pursue their dreams. I was amazed to read the story of oceanographer Slava Kurilov. Having realized he had no chance of pursuing his dream of exploring the ocean if he stayed in the Soviet Union, he escaped by jumping off a ship near the Philippines and swimming for three days and nights to get ashore. His description of those three days in the deep tropical phosphorescent waters sounds like something out of a dream.

The tendency to escapism along with the demographic changes in the late 1960s–1970s (this was the time of one-child families where both parents worked, living in big cities) gave birth to a number of cartoons about lonely characters. In another famous cartoon, *Cheburashka*, Gena the Crocodile for some reason finds himself all on his own and has to advertize for friends. Another cartoon of the times is *The Mitten*, about a girl who imagines her mitten turning into the puppy she so ardently wishes for. And in *Hedgehog in the Mist*, as Hedgehog is walking through the woods mumbling to himself imagining a conversation with Bear Cub, we get the sensation that maybe Bear Cub does not exist at all, maybe he is actually an imaginary friend, and Hedgehog lives entirely in the world of his imagination.

❄❄❄

In Kozlov's stories, Hedgehog is the most spiritual member of the bunch. He can close his eyes and hear the frog singing. Bear Cub tries to do the same, but however near he stands to Hedgehog hoping to hear the frog, he cannot.

Bear Cub is a carer. He is the most responsive to his friends' needs. He is the one who constantly lights up the samovar, and always has in his larder some fruit preserve, mushrooms, berries or honey. Hare's friends think he is a bit unimaginative. But when spring comes, he can do pretty crazy things, like running around at tremendous speed pretending he is a spring breeze.

My favourite story is about Hare asking to watch the twilight with Hedgehog and Bear Cub. In Russian it is called *Разрешите с вами посумерничать*. There is an old English word, darkling, for this, as in: "Let us sit darkling together" – though I prefer the translation *Let Me Watch the Twilight With You*. Reading this story recently, I almost jumped at the beauty of this word. Living abroad for quite a few years, and most of the time speaking languages other than your native tongue, you do not notice how words from your native language slowly slip into oblivion. But from time to time you read a book, and you see a word that is so precise and evocative, and you think – gosh, when was the last time I used this word? Years ago. It is like a long lost friend, partly but not entirely forgotten, who suddenly appears in front of you.

"Sumernichat" comes from "sumerki" – twilight. It is a verb that means to sit through the evening without light, as it gets dark. There is more to it though – it has overtones of good company, unforced conversation, comfortable silence, slowly darkening landscape, your friends turning into dark shadows so you can hardly see them, but feel their warmth... Enjoying the long warm evenings of the short Russian summer. And if you are also drinking tea from an old samovar, one that has a space underneath the water tank to fill with twigs and pine cones and light up, so that the tea smells of wood and smoke, and in a little glass bowl you have some home-made fruit *varenye*...

Kozlov's stories have an interesting relationship with time. Time passes and the forest is always changing, but there is a quiet, almost oriental stillness in the characters' attitude to time.

"We talk and talk, and the days fly by, and still we keep talking....
–We keep talking," agreed the Hedgehog. "Months pass by, the clouds fly past, the trees are bare, and we keep chatting."
– Our chats.
– And later everything will pass, and only two of us remain.
– If only!
– What will become of us?
– We can also fly away.

– Like birds?
– Aha.
– But where to?
– To the South, - said Hedgehog."

It is clear why Yuri Norstein chose Kozlov's story for his film. There is a playfulness about space and light in his animation, in the same way as Kozlov plays with time in his stories. Norstein says: "For me the light is a character in the film. It is flesh, substance, the immaterial world… When I was a child, I lived in a communal flat. There was a long corridor there, and the blinding sun cut through its shadows. I still remember the feeling of my heart trembling – you are about to step over that threshold, into the light, into a different world."

Norstein is an enigmatic Russian soul. Or rather, an enigmatic Jewish Russian soul, which is quite possibly an enigmatic Russian soul magnified. In his work, he does not accept such innovations as computer animation. When Swedish animators asked him how he manages to convey so well the feeling of three-dimensional space, the director told them he and his team do not wipe the camera lenses. Apart from possibly being true, this answer is reminiscent of all those jokes Russians make about themselves, where a foreigner, usually an American or a German, asks a Russian how he achieves such magnificent results, only to get the answer that it is by doing less rather than more, or by accident.

But the effect of space in Norstein's films and the expressiveness of his characters are also due to the special technique that he uses, that includes superimposing layers of celluloid and moving minute parts of the picture by hand for each frame. His animation is truly artisanal. His tools are paper, sheets of celluloid, sellotape, pencils, scissors, a stand, light, cameras and tweezers (my computer, Norstein calls them), which he uses to move the tiny pieces that form part of the picture to be filmed.

The immediately recognizable style of Norstein's films was created in collaboration with his long-standing team, among whom are his wife Francesca Yarbusova, who is the lead artist in his films, and cameraman Alexander Zhukovsky, who sadly died recently. The basic technique is that of the "flat puppet", one of the classical animation techniques.

Someone once commented to Norstein that there is an impression that he consciously limits his creative possibilities, just so as to have to overcome the obstacles. Norstein replied that "when there are fewer possibilities, the creative catalyst… the brain, the fantasy, start working more actively. I am afraid of limitless possibilities." He also said: "Technology must resist what you have invented". Norstein is famous for being a tyrant at work, particularly towards his wife Francesca. Norstein said that as soon as Francesca's drawings become too beautiful and self-admiring, he demands that she starts drawing with her left hand.

Francesca Yarbusova talks of how a film is made. For example a St Petersburg street is drawn on paper. Then it is photographed. Then she has to rub the windows on the piece of celluloid, so that they become transparent, and when a lamp is put behind them, the effect of light coming from the windows is achieved. She emphasizes the shadows with black ink. On top of it all, she sprinkles the celluloid picture with water from her fingertips, to create shimmering effect. Or when drawing a forest, to create an impression of late autumn with "traces, patches of grass, bushes with few remaining leaves", she had to rub through kilometres of celluloid, until her fingers began to shake.

Norstein is seen as an enigmatic genius. His films are few, the main ones being: *Fox and Hare* (1973), *Heron and Crane* (1974), *Hedgehog in the Mist* (1975) and *Tale of Tales* (1979). What also makes him conform to the myth of a hermit artist, not quite belonging to this world, is the fact that for over twenty years the director has been working on the same project, an animated film based on Nikolai Gogol's nineteenth-century story *The Overcoat*. In this story, a harmless St Petersburg clerk notices he is losing the respect of his colleagues because of his very old and shabby overcoat; he spends months saving up to have a new one made, and is robbed of it as he goes home late after a party that has been thrown to celebrate his new garment. When he asks an important person for help, he gets scolded so badly that he falls sick and dies. Later on his ghost starts troubling the people of St Petersburg, trying to steal their coats…

This story has been interpreted in many different ways and had a huge influence on Gogol's contemporaries. Fyodor Dostoyevsky famously said "We all came out from under Gogol's *Overcoat*".

"The horror I felt when I read Gogol for the first time is still alive in me," says Norstein. "The horror of a teenager." This horror was born from the phrase: "Leave me alone, why are you hurting me?"

A child, not an adult, could say such a thing, says Norstein: "and in my childhood this discrepancy between the character and the word made a bigger impression on me than the story of the stolen overcoat and the dead clerk."

Another of Norstein's old memories is the atmosphere in which he first discovered Gogol. He spent his childhood in a communal flat in a two-storey house in Moscow whose windows overlooked a textile factory. The factory worked non-stop, and the noise was constant. Norstein was mesmerized by the gigantic looms he could see through his windows, and the female workers pacing along them. He found the scene both terrifying and irresistible. He watched the factory out of his window, as the street got dark, lit only by a few dim street lights shimmering under the metal shades. "The light was making something stand out in the cold darkness – and this was terrifying..." "I could not get away from the window, where everything was sinking into darkness. Those lamps with metallic shades, shadows, perspective..."

The Overcoat remains a work in progress, and only a few episodes have been shown at gatherings of animators. In a documentary about Norstein, you see him working on the film, in the studio full of drawers where celluloid parts of the characters are kept, marked, for example, "Akaky's hands" or "Noses". Using tweezers, he puts them together, and moves them by hand, for each frame, thus achieving that incredible expressiveness of faces (and also hands, and even toes).

The slow pace of filming *The Overcoat* is not only due to the director's perfectionism and the laborious artisanal style of working, but also the lack of funds, and the disruptions of the transitional period in Russia. Still, twenty-plus years is a long time to be filming one animated cartoon film.

On one occasion an interviewer asked Norstein if the director was scared not to have enough time to finish the work of his life. Norstein answered: "This is a normal feeling for anyone. Back when I was working on *The Hedgehog in the Mist*, I was 34 and I could not get rid of this feeling."

A statue of Hedgehog (in the mist) was erected in Kiev in January 2009. He sits on the bole of a tree, with the same round mouth and eyes full of wonder as in the cartoon, and in his paws he is holding a small bundle, containing, most probably, a jar of raspberry jam...

Language notes:

"По вечерам Ёжик ходил к Медвежонку считать звёзды. Они усаживались на брёвнышке и, прихлёбывая чай, смотрели на звёздное небо. Оно висело над крышей — прямо за печной трубой. Справа от трубы были звёзды Медвежонка, а слева — Ёжика…" – "In the evening Hedgehog went to Bear Cub's house to count stars. They sat on a tree log, and sipped at their tea, looking at the starry sky. It hung over the roof – right behind the chimney. On the right of the chimney were Bear Cub's stars, and on the left Hedgehog's…"

"Вот. И даже лапы не видно…" – "Here. I can't even see my own paw…"

"Я в реке, пускай река сама несёт меня", — решил Ёжик, как мог глубоко вздохнул, и его понесло вниз по течению. – "I am in the river, let it carry me," –Hedgehog decided, and took the deepest breath he could, as the current was taking him down

"Я совсем промок, я скоро утону." – I am completely soaked. I will soon drown."

"Я Ёжик. Я упал в реку." – "I am Hedgehog. I fell into the river."

"Ведь кто же, кроме тебя, звёзды-то считать будет?!" – "If not you, who is going to count stars?"

Медвежонок говорил, говорил, а Ёжик думал: "Всё-таки хорошо, что мы снова вместе". И ещё Ёжик думал о Лошади: "Как она там, в тумане?" – "Bear Cub was talking, and talking, and Hedgehog was thinking: 'It is really good that we are together again.' And Hedgehog was also thinking about Horse: 'How is she out there, in the mist?'"

It is worth mentioning here that ёжик /hedgehog is also a hairstyle that can be a crew-cut, or slightly longer spiky hair.

SHERLOCK HOLMES AND DR WATSON

ШЕРЛОК ХОЛМС И ДОКТОР ВАТСОН

The year was 1979, Leonid Brezhnev's eyebrows were getting more and more unruly and his speech more and more slurred, the period later known as the "Era of Stagnation" was at its most turgid, and Soviet troops were about to enter Afghanistan. Russians' enthusiasm for Soviet ideology was low, and their interest in what was happening on the other side of the Iron Curtain was high. The public was listening avidly through the crackles to foreign radio stations broadcasting into the USSR, and the inventing and telling of politically-charged jokes in the company of friends was turned into an art form.

Against this background Lenfilm, the Leningrad film studio, was digging around in its warehouses for any furniture and fittings that could help recreate the atmosphere of Victorian England, or to be more precise, the furnishings in one famous set of lodgings at 221B Baker Street, London.

The Sherlock Holmes series was made between 1979 and 1986, and consists of five series, each in two, or on one occasion three, episodes.

The screenplays were written by Valery Frid and Yuly Dunsky. The destinies of these two authors, who became friends while at school together, stayed interwoven throughout their lives, like those of Sherlock Holmes and Dr Watson. They both studied at the Moscow Film Institute (VGIK), and in 1940 both were arrested on political charges. They met each other again in the Gulag. When rehabilitated (after ten years in forced-labour camps), they came back to Moscow to finish their studies. They always wrote their scripts together, and by the late 1970s the fruit of their collaboration was very much in demand, so they would not usually write something without having a "buyer" already waiting. But in this case, in their spare time and for their own pleasure, they produced the script of *The Adventures of Sherlock Holmes and Doctor Watson* and presented it to the film director Igor Maslennikov.

And that's how it all started. The director, who had to persuade the artistic committee (in Soviet reality, a combination of producers and censors) of his choice of actors, used Sydney Paget's drawings to justify his casting of Vasily Livanov as Holmes. As for Dr Watson, comparing photos of Vitaly Solomin with the pictures of the young Conan Doyle cemented the decision to use the actor for this role. While for Russian audiences Vasily Livanov *is* Sherlock Holmes, he has also been acknowledged among Sherlockians in the English-speaking world, and even by the British monarchy, which in 2006 awarded the actor an honorary MBE for his contribution to popularizing British culture.

Livanov's Holmes is humorous, enthusiastic to the point of being childlike, mischievous and passionate. At the same time he is, naturally, also intense and rational. He can be destructive and is prone to practising his shooting in the apartment when he is bored, and making screeching sounds on his violin when concentrating intensely. But he is not as self-destructive as the original, since portraying Holmes on Soviet TV as a drug-user was completely out of the question. Possibly through avoiding unhealthy habits, apart from pipe-smoking, the Russian Holmes is not as aloof or moody as the original. He is also louder and less reserved. His good physical condition is shown in a non-canonical episode in the first series, when he and Watson engage in a sparring session, and Holmes knocks the doctor giddy, despite Watson's claim that he was regimental champion in his weight class.

What is particular about the Russian Sherlock Holmes is his voice, which is quite unique and immediately recognizable to all Russians. Vasily Livanov likes to tell the story of his voice. He used to have a normal baritone, until as a young actor he participated in an experimental film that was made in the middle of the Siberian winter, and with the director trying to record the voices live, rather than doing studio-based "looping". As a result of trying to outshout the howling Siberian snowstorms, Livanov lost his voice for a couple of weeks. When he was able to speak again he realized, to his horror, that his voice had completely changed, and forever retained this hoarse quality, that was to become his (and, for Russians, Sherlock Holmes's) trademark.

As for Dr Watson... the director Maslennikov admitted that without Vitaly Solomin, the series would not be the same. Sherlock Holmes – whoever plays him – must remain an exotic, eccentric character, but Solomin as Watson brings the human dimension that makes this series so engaging. Many Sherlockian bloggers agree that Vitaly Solomin is the true star of this film, and call him the best

Watson ever (some also refer to him as being "ridiculously hot"). Quintessentially Russian in his other movies, Solomin, who grew up in a wooden house in southeast Siberia, is very convincing as the young English military doctor. He is subtle and warm, but also firm and obstinate. He is loyal, has a splendidly stiff upper lip, but is also touchingly emotional. He can be ironic, but most of the time is tirelessly amazed at his friend's deductive skills. With him, plots that could have been rather far-fetched become quite believable.

Rina Zelenaya, a versatile actress who was in her 80s, makes a delightful Mrs Hudson, and her exaggerated take on the British ability to remain unperturbed along with her grand manner add a deliberate comic dimension.

As for Professor Moriarty, he lacks the subtlety of George Zucco in the Basil Rathbone *Sherlock Holmes* series. He is a bit like a villain from a children's film, enough to give you nightmares – you don't even know what he's done or why. He is tall but slightly hunched, dressed in shiny black, has a white face, limbs like tentacles, and as if that wasn't enough, he likes to writhe his gloved fingers about like snakes, particularly when going for the Holmes throat in the famous scene at the Reichenbach falls.

And then there is the immediately recognizable music, although it is perhaps overused in the series. The director tried to inspire the composer Vladimir Dashkevich by playing him the signature tune of the BBC Russian Service on the phone, having previously recorded it on a dictaphone – and that's how the melody familiar to all Russians was born.

The Russian series is generally faithful to what Sherlockians call "the canon". Sometimes several stories are combined into one, but it feels seamless.

There is great attention to detail, both in following the Conan Doyle stories and in recreating the atmosphere of Victorian London. Luckily for Lenfilm, their warehouses were full of furniture and other bits and bobs of aristocratic life expropriated during the revolution from the rich houses of St Petersburg. The designers used photos from the Sherlock Holmes Museum in London to recreate the interior. For the outside scenes, Riga, St Petersburg and their surrounding areas provided the "non-Russian" (if not exactly London) feel. Luckily, the city on the Neva river has no shortage of fog, and cunning camera angles in the misty darkness cut only by shimmering gaslights achieved the spooky London-of-Jack-the-Ripper effect. It was on the Neva that the boat chase in *The Sign of Four* was shot. In the Conan Doyle story the steam launch in which the villains were escaping was called the *Aurora*. You might also remember that the Neva has its own *Aurora*, the legendary ship whose guns on 25 October 1917 were the signal for the attack on the Winter Palace and beginning of the October revolution. Any schoolchild in Soviet Russia knew about that *Aurora* (which is now a museum, moored near the Winter Palace), and the idea of Sherlock Holmes chasing it was not acceptable, so the name was changed for the Russian series.

Another deviation from Conan Doyle that had to be made for political reasons was when Holmes asks Watson in the very first episode: "How long ago did you come back from Afghanistan?" (in the original : "You have been in Afghanistan, I perceive"). The censorship committee that evaluated the film before releasing it to the public almost fainted when they heard this phrase, since Soviet troops had just entered Afghanistan. The phrase had to be changed to "How long ago did you come back from the East?"

Apart from the politically-motivated changes, the makers of the film felt the need to correct Conan Doyle's mistake in *The Speckled Band*, where Roylott calls the snake by whistling. As snakes actually rely on ground vibration for hearing, Holmes and Watson suggest that Roylott used tapping as well as whistling, to double check the snake heard the call. While filming, they also found out that snakes do not go up or down a free hanging rope, so the snake in the film is shown crawling out of the ventilation hatch.

The series had tremendous success and provoked an outbreak of Sherlockmania, with plot developments being discussed on public transport and in school canteens. As the "Era of Stagnation" was also a golden age for folk humour, plenty of jokes appeared, affectionately making fun of the immortal detective and his loyal Dr Watson.

The Sherlock Holmes series allowed Soviet people to travel vicariously. One has to remember that the vast majority of Russians who were watching it in the 1970s and early 1980s were convinced they would never, ever be able to go and see Baker Street with their own eyes. "Abroad" seemed – and was – so inaccessible that there was a joke that the outside world simply did not exist, and when someone from the Soviet Union thought he went "abroad", he was in fact being taken by the KGB to some artificially created town, built to resemble

New York, Rome or Paris somewhere in the plains of Kazakhstan. Tragic as it was, living in a world of stereotypes without the opportunity to encounter the much more complicated realities of different countries was actually comforting and convenient. The "abroad" was created on the TV to match the stereotypes Russians had about other nations, and it was much easier to think of London as having a lot of fog and filled with English gentlemen wearing bowler hats than it is now to fathom the multicultural UK. Now the world before globalization evokes nostalgia, and in a funny kind of way, even the Iron Curtain is missed. Although Russians do travel now, there seem to be – at least in Moscow – a remarkable number of groups of people with an interest in a particular foreign culture, be it flamenco, Irish dancing, African drumming or Argentine tango. Of course this happens everywhere, but in Moscow it seems more so. And Russians who participate in these groups pay extraordinary attention to achieving maximum authenticity, whether it's imitating an Andalusian accent when singing flamenco, or learning elvian to better understand Tolkien. Maybe those thematic cultural enclaves are created to compensate for the physical distance from other countries and the lack of a multicultural society.

Escapism was definitely part of the success of *Sherlock Holmes*. Victorian Britain, credited with "inventing childhood", somehow resonated with the infantilism of the "Era of Stagnation". There was a great demand for works of art into which one could escape, where one could feel protected and peaceful, and at the same time free to explore the world, like a well-looked-after child. English children's writers such as Lewis Carroll and A.A. Milne were very popular in the USSR, not only with children, but also with adults. Were readers in the Soviet Union, where education placed great emphasis on maths and technical sciences (I have mentioned the profusion of engineers) attracted by those authors' – both mathematicians – playful attitude to logic? Their imagination and the free flight of fancy? Was their ironic tone welcome in a society in which irony was lacking and the government was completely devoid of any sense of humour? (Despite being humourless, the authorities from time to time gave us a good laugh, as in one typical address to schoolchildren that said: "Every A grade you get in maths is like a rocket fired at the Pentagon").

Some researchers even went as far as comparing Victorian Britain and Brezhnev's USSR. It would be hard to justify such comparison.

Could the Victorian age be known as the "Era of Stagnation"? There was at least one similarity, though: compared to the eras of Stalin and Khrushchev, Brezhnev's time was certainly one of stability and (relatively) increased affluence. It's also seen like that in retrospect, compared to the upheavals that came afterwards. But the curious thing about Russia is that stability is always contrasted to freedom, as though the two cannot possibly exist together. The basic ideology underpinning Vladimir Putin and his United Russia party is the idea of stability, and making people scared of the supposed alternative: renewed social and economic upheaval, crime and the disintegration of the state. One of the fascinating things about Victorian Britain for the Russians is to see that stability, prosperity and freedom can actually coexist perfectly well.

Essayist Alexander Genis highlights the "perfection of the social machine" in the Sherlock Holmes stories: "Everything there works the way we would like it to work. The letter that was sent in the morning reaches its addressee by the afternoon with the same inevitability with which the investigation reveals the motive of the crime, Holmes finds Moriarty and any problem gets solved." "Sherlock Holmes and Dr Watson are guarding the grave of that beautiful world which was based on Law and Order, where the two were one," he says, adding "the hidden protagonist of Conan Doyle's stories is the civilized world".

I think Soviet viewers were attracted to the maverick quality of Sherlock Holmes. First of all, in the USSR, of course, there were no private detectives. So it was fascinating to see how someone could do something like this as a job. Secondly, Holmes worked alone, outside the official forces of law and order; staying in the shadows while the police took all the glory. This created the aura of a hero and, almost, a "dissident" around his persona, someone living outside the "system". His detachment from everyday routine helped viewers detach themselves from their daily drudgery.

Holmes is also the personification of some sort of supreme justice. He is someone who never makes a mistake, never confuses the victim and the perpetrator, the innocent person and the villain. In a world where official justice was not seen as being able to protect you, here was some higher authority to turn to, as a last resort. Besides, his justice is human justice, not state justice. And his behaviour, as well as Dr Watson's, is always gentlemanly beyond reproach.

Another reason for the series' success was Russians' fascination with "Englishness", as they perceive it. As director Maslennikov said: "In reality this is not England at all. It is England the way we imagined it." The director and the actors were "playing at being English", Maslennikov said, and thoroughly enjoying it. And the viewers were thoroughly enjoying watching it.

As I write this, I remember my first couple of years in England, with my Russian friends and us all also playing at being English. How exciting it was to sit down near a newly-restored fireplace, and stoke the glowing logs with a vintage poker bought at Portobello market. To drive around the countryside in an old blue Land Rover. How special strawberries and cream once tasted...

The history of "anglophilia" is long in Russia, though I will resist going on a historical detour, as it would require too much space.

Remember Turgenev's *Fathers and Sons*, with its depiction of two landowners, one an anglophile (he wears crisp white collars in the middle of the countryside, and he admires English political traditions), the other a "slavophile", who prefers to dwell on his "Russianness". Remember, too, Vladimir Nabokov's father, the politician who dressed as a London dandy, and whose son learnt to read English before he learnt to read Russian, subsequently becoming one of the great stylists of both Russian and English literature.

But what I really like is the following episode from the nineteenth-century novel *Oblomov* by Goncharov. In this novel the hero is a lazy, inert landowner who once had his share of ideas and aspirations but lost them all, sucked into the torpor of provincial life. His friend, a Russian German called Stoltz, comes to try to rouse him out of his wallowing. Laughing at Oblomov's laziness, Stoltz calls his friend a real Russian *"barin"* – the form of address of the peasants to their landowner. Oblomov protests and says there is no difference between a Russian *barin* and an English gentleman. Stoltz disagrees, saying an English gentleman puts on his own socks and takes off his own boots (while a Russian *barin* lies down on a bed and lets his servants do it).

I think this difference is something that is lodged into Russians' notion of "the English", whom they still prefer to imagine as invariably white, educated aristocrats, never really having fathomed either the reality of multicultural UK nor the division between North and South; England, Scotland and Wales; Kensington and Tottenham.

"An English gentleman" or an "English lady" for anglophile Russians is like a magic mirror in which they would like to see themselves. A country in which an aristocrat takes off his own boots must have reached a different level of civilization, a different level of social consciousness and respect for oneself and others, they think.

Britain is so fascinating for the Russians because it represents, more than other cultures, what is most absent in Russia: calm self-respect and conservatism coupled with independence of spirit and self-assurance. More importantly still, it has Habeas corpus, the rights of an individual versus the authorities, an unshakable respect for property and private life and the sanctity of the law.

Sending their kids to British schools, rich Russians are hoping to install their children into this established, secure, solid world of traditions. At the same time, "Moscow-on-Thames" became a safe haven for Russian plutocrats, thanks to the UK's peculiar oligarch-friendly tax regime.

Speaking of this interest in England, Conan Doyle was also very popular in Russia during his lifetime. Nicholas II, for example, read *The Hound of the Baskervilles* in 1917, just as a terrible fate was hovering over his own doomed dynasty and family.

But there is also something ironic about the Russians' view of England. Maybe it is because even Russian Anglophiles understand that the England of their imagination is just too comfortable and too good to be true.

The Russian *Sherlock Holmes* series always had a bit of a tongue-in-cheek quality, and by the time the ensemble started filming *The Hound of the Baskervilles*, the comic element had reached a peak. Watch Henry Baskerville (those who have seen a few Russian movies will recognize Nikita Mikhalkov, the star and director of *Burnt by the Sun*) slap his head in fury with his remaining shoe, the other having been stolen from his hotel... The Russian Sir Henry is meant to be an open, loud North American who likes to eat steak, even for breakfast. What he tends to get at Baskerville Hall though, is porridge – served by Barrymore with the words "Porridge, sir" – that he is obviously not so crazy about. It is not clear whether it is the hound, the unrequited love, or the excess of porridge that most bothers him at his ancestral seat. The situation becomes particularly comical when Mrs Barrymore feeds him porridge while he is in bed recovering from his encounter with the hound.

This "porridge, sir", has etched itself firmly into the minds of Russians, who associate it with England. It also gave rise to many jokes, as did the series in general (see language notes).

Now, of course, Russians can compare and contrast their own beloved Livanov with other interpretations of the world's most famous detective. The new BBC series starring Benedict Cumberbatch reached Russian TV almost immediately after it had been broadcast in the UK, and Russian viewers have also seen Jeremy Brett's brilliantly original Holmes. But guess who is still the all-time favourite?

Language notes:

"Это же элементарно, Ватсон!" – "Elementary, Watson!"

"Что это, Бэрримор? — Овсянка, сэр." — "What is this, Barrymore? — Porridge, sir."

Here are some of the jokes ("anekdoty" in Russian) about Sherlock Holmes and Dr Watson inspired by the series:

"— Бэрримор, что у меня хлюпает в ботинке?
— Овсянка, сэр.
— *Овсянка?!* А что она там делает?
— Хлюпает, сэр."

"— Barrymore, what is that slurping about in my shoe?
— Porridge, sir.
— *Porridge?* What is porridge doing in my shoe?
— Slurping about, sir."

"Сэр Баскервиль зовет Бэрримора:
— Бэрримор, а что у нас на завтрак?
— Овсянка, сэр.
— А что у нас на обед?
— Овсянка, сэр.
— Ээ, ага, а на ужин?
— Котлеты, сэр
— УРАААА!!!!!!!!!!!!!!!!!!!!!!
— Шутка, сэр"

"— Barrymore, what are we having for breakfast?
— Porridge, sir.
— And what are we having for lunch?
— Porridge, sir.
— Eh… and for dinner?
— Cutlets, sir.
— Hooray!
— Joke, sir."

Гуляя по болотам, Шерлок Холмс с Ватсоном слышат ужасный вой. Ватсон спрашивает Холмса:
— Холмс, это воет собака Баскервилей?
— Нет, Ватсон, невозмутимо отвечает Холмс, — это Бэрримор кормит сэра Генри овсянкой.

Walking around the moors, Sherlock Holmes and Dr Watson hear a terrible howling. Watson asks Holmes:
— Holmes, is that the hound howling?
— No, Watson – Holmes replies nonchalantly – that is Barrymore feeding porridge to Sir Henry.

— Ватсон, а что это вы курите? Давайте угадаю – табак "Королева Вирджиния" с листочками вишни, из юбилейного выпуска в бархатной упаковке?
— Поразительно, Холмс! Как это вы угадали?
— Ей-богу, Ватсон! Ну не миссис Хадсон же стырила из моей комнаты последнюю пачку!

— Watson, what are you smoking? Let me guess – Queen Virginia with cherry leaves, jubilee issue, comes in a velvet box?
— This is amazing, Holmes! How did you guess?
— Really, Watson! It couldn't have been Mrs Hudson who pinched the last packet from my room!

Some jokes show that despite making Holmes clean-living in the Russian series, Russians were aware of the detective's drug use:

— Холмс, а вы и правда видели собаку Баскервилей?
(Холмс, протягивая Ватсону трубку):
— Попробуйте, Ватсон, вы и не такое увидите!

— Holmes, have you really seen the hound of the Baskervilles?
(Holmes, handing his pipe to Watson):
— Try this Watson, and you will see even more amazing things!

— Холмс, как вы думаете, почему фиолетовое лицо, которое плавает по воздуху в нашей гостиной, корчит мне такие страшные рожи?
— Я думаю, Ватсон, оно сердится потому, что это был МОЙ кокаин.

— Holmes, why do you think the purple head that is floating around our living room is making such scary faces at me?
— I think, Watson, it is angry, because it was MY cocaine.

CPSIA information can be obtained at www.ICGtesting.com
Printed in the USA
LVOW12s0722271013

358717LV00005B/522/P